Barrie Mahoney worked as a teacher and head teacher in the south west of England, and then became a school inspector in England and Wales. A new life and career as a newspaper reporter in Spain's Costa Blanca led to him launching and editing an English language newspaper in the Canary Islands. Barrie's books include novels in 'The Prior's Hill Chronicles' series, as well as books for expats in the 'Twitters from the Atlantic' series, which give an amusing and reflective view of life abroad.

Barrie writes regular columns for newspapers and magazines in Spain, Portugal, Ireland, Australia, South Africa, Canada, UK and the USA. He also designs mobile apps and websites to promote the Canary Islands and expat life, and is often asked to contribute to radio programmes about expat life.

Visit the author's websites:

www.barriemahoney.com
www.thecanaryislander.com

Other books by Barrie Mahoney

Journeys & Jigsaws (The Canary Islander Publishing) 2013
ISBN: 978 184386 646 6 (Paperback and eBook)

Threads and Threats (The Canary Islander Publishing) 2013
ISBN: 978 184386 645 9 (Paperback and eBook)

Letters from the Atlantic (The Canary Islander Publishing) 2013
ISBN: 978-0992767136 (Paperback and eBook)

Living the Dream (The Canary Islander Publishing) 2011
ISBN: 978 145076 704 0 (Paperback and eBook)

Expat Survival (The Canary Islander Publishing) 2012
ISBN: 978-1479130481 (Paperback and eBook)

Message in a Bottle (The Canary Islander Publishing) 2012
ISBN: 978-1480031005 (Paperback and eBook)

Twitters from the Atlantic (The Canary Islander Publishing) 2012
ISBN: 978-1480033986 (Paperback and eBook)

Escape to the Sun (The Canary Islander Publishing) 2013
ISBN: 978-0957544444 (Paperback and eBook)

Expat Voice (The Canary Islander Publishing) 2014
ISBN: 978-0992767174 (Paperback and eBook)

Island in the Sun

Barrie Mahoney

The Canary Islander Publishing

© Copyright 2015

Barrie Mahoney

The right of Barrie Mahoney to be identified as author of this work has been asserted by him in accordance with the Copyright, Designs and Patents Act 1988.

All Rights Reserved

No reproduction, copy or transmission of this publication may be made without written permission. No paragraph of this publication may be reproduced, copied or transmitted save with the written permission of the author, or in accordance with the provisions of the Copyright Act 1956 (as amended).
Any person who commits any unauthorised act in relation to this publication may be liable to criminal prosecution and civil claims for damages.
A CIP catalogue record for this title is available from the British Library.

ISBN 978-0992767181
www.barriemahoney.com

First Published in 2015

The Canary Islander Publishing

Acknowledgements

I would like to thank all those people that I have met on my journey to where I am now.

To supportive friends who helped me to overcome the many problems and frustrations that I faced and taught me much about learning to adapt to a new culture. Also, to friends in the UK, or scattered around the world, who have kept in touch despite being so far away.

To the people that I met whilst working as a newspaper reporter and editor in Spain and the Canary Islands, and for the privilege of sharing their successes and challenges in life.

Disclaimer

This is a book about real people, real places and real events, but names of people and companies have been changed to avoid any embarrassment.

DEDICATION

This book is dedicated to expats all over the world who dream of a new life, new experiences, new cultures, new opportunities to experience, taste and smell the excitement of a place that is of their own choosing and not merely based upon an accident of birth.

Contents	10
Preface	13
Island in the Sun	16
Looking Local	20
Just Call Me Scruffy	21
Wearing a Dress to Make a Point	23
No More Tossers in Tossa del Mar	26
Sunshine, Cactus and Roses	29
Strawberries, Cheese and the White Bottomed Bumble Bee	32
A Bit of a Storm – a reality check	35
112 – Emergency, Emergency	38
Getting Political	41
Expats Are Migrants Too	42
The Solidarity Fridge	45
Keeping the Vote	48
The Scourge of Meetings	50
Let Them Eat Gold!	53
Oil Slicks, Turtles and Lies	56
Joining In	59
That Eurovision Feeling	60
Playing the Game	63
Kisses, Cuddles and Coffee	67
The Birthday Expat	70
The Unfriendly Expat	73

Healthy, Wealthy and Wise?	76
The Atlantic Travelling Butter Dish	77
Drinking Foggy Water	80
Healthcare for Expats in Spain and the Canary Islands	82
Fight Alzheimer's – Learn a Language!	85
Go on, Unzip a Banana!	88
Open Wide!	91
Money Doesn't Buy Happiness, But It Helps	93

Boys' and Girls' Toys	96
Boys' Toys	97
Techie Toys for Expats: Stay Smart with DNS	99
Twitter Town	102
The Viewfinder Blues	105
Viaduct Power	108

Party Time	111
The Non-designer Christmas Tree	112
Pancakes, Vicars and Tarts	115
Wine and Sex in the Canary Islands	118
Island Pride	121
A Bit of a Do	124

Buzzing Around	127
"Love Me, Love My Thorax"	128
Robins and Canaries	130
Barbeque or What?	133
The Disgruntled Expat	135
Strictly at the Bus Station	139
Travelling Back in Time	142

Lavender Lemonade and Biscuits	144
The Robinson Crusoe Experience	147
Beware of Visitors Wearing Black and Yellow Striped Shirts	149
There's Nothing Grotty About Lanzarote!	151
How Not To Do It	153
"We're All-inclusive" – Set Yourself Free!	154
What an Inconvenience!	157
Boozing Whilst Cruising	159
The End of the World?	162

Preface

Preface

When I published 'Letters from the Atlantic' five years ago, I thought that would be the end of it. It was meant to be an account of part of my life, and intended to inspire other people to take control of their lives and head towards a life in the sun. It was an account of my dreams, and the delights and challenges that helped to turn my dream into reality.

We do not have to head to an 'Island in the Sun' to fulfil our dreams. It can be wherever we wish; whatever we envisage to be our own personal paradise. It may be a villa in a Spanish village, an apartment in a French town, or a semi detached in North Wales. The important thing is that it is where we have chosen to be and that we have taken control of our own lives, and not just where we are programmed or expected to be. Life is short and we need to take control.

Since that book was published, I have received many requests from would be and existing expats for more information and help about their life in the sun, and it is always a privilege to help when I can. Some questions are easy to answer, whilst others are challenging and sometimes worrying. Answers to many of these questions, as well as accounts of the challenges that I faced as a newly arrived expat were eventually published in a series of 'Twitters from the Atlantic', 'Letters from the Atlantic' and 'Twitters from Spain' in a number of publications in several countries.

Later, I began to be asked for back copies of articles with worryingly titles, such as 'Death in Spain' and 'Wills and Inheritance' being some of the most popular requests. It soon became easier to put all the articles into a book at the end of the year, which would provide easy access to the weekly 'Letters'.

Five years on, 'Island in the Sun', is the latest book that offers advice and suggestions, as well as revealing some of the mistakes that I have made as an expat living in Spain and the Canary Islands. Some stories are 'tongue in cheek' reflections of a life that I sometimes find challenging, as well as exciting.

Although I now live in the Canary Islands, I continue to receive emails from many expats living in Spain, as well as other countries, and many of the stories are based upon conversations with people that I have never met. We all have one thing in common; we are all trying to fulfil our own dreams, yet we do not have to live on an island to create our own 'Island in the Sun'.

Island in the Sun

I can still remember when my passion for islands began. As a small boy, I was standing with my Great Aunt Gertie on Poole Harbour looking across the short distance of water to a mysterious island. It was called Brownsea Island, and it was a place where no one had visited for many years. Aunt Gertie, always a good storyteller, captured my imagination with her story of a lonely, cross, old woman who lived in the castle, with only her gardener for company. She was something called a "recluse", which according to my Aunt Gertie meant that she didn't like people and wanted to be on her own. I listened in wonder, as my Aunt continued with her story about the island being bombed by the German Luftwaffe during the Second World War. She continued her story of the island being the home of a budding pottery industry, and the deaf woman who was instrumental in bringing the island business crashing down, and the bankruptcy that followed.

I still vividly remember that first afternoon, which was the seed that led me to devour stories about islands for many years. Books such as 'The Famous Five', 'Swallows and Amazons' and 'Robinson Crusoe' fed my growing imagination during those formative years; the more islands the better.

It was many years later when I revisited Poole Harbour that I discovered that the old woman who owned Brownsea Island had died, and that the island was now in the care of the National Trust, with the John Lewis Partnership leasing and managing the castle. It was now possible to visit the island on a day trip, and I would discover for the first time if the castle was really haunted, as Aunt Gertie had implied.

I never did discover or indeed go inside the castle, other than the tearoom many years later, but I did spend many happy years as a teacher visiting the island with parties of chattering school children, who seemed to delight in the wonder of stories of this beautiful island in much the same way that I did as a child many years earlier. I recall the look of wonder on the faces of many seven-year-olds as they discovered "giant ants", met peacocks in all their splendour for the first time, discovered the occasional red squirrel if they were particularly quiet, and explored the very first scout camp that Baden Powell established. The highlight of such visits was always a picnic lunch on 'Pottery Pier' as the children discovered pieces of old brown pottery, which were remnants of the small pottery industry that began on the island and spectacularly crashed many years ago. Brownsea Island found a place in my heart that remains there to this very day.

For many years, I had known that one day I would live on an island. My first overseas holiday was on the island of Capri, which was my first taste of an island in the sun. Later, I found myself drawn to many islands off the coast of Britain, particularly those off the west and north coasts of Scotland, such as Orkney, Shetland, Mull, Harris, Lewis, the Uists and many others. As much as I appreciated the many whisky distilleries that we visited, as well as some spectacular scenery, the cold and damp were not for us. We also visited the Isles of Scilly, which was where I finally realised that islands involve water and boats, and as I was not a good sailor, the Scilly Isles were clearly not for me either, as delightful as they were.

Later in my career, when I was looking for my first headship, I applied for a job on the Isle of Wight. Over a number of years, my partner and I had grown to appreciate this peaceful island, and getting there was certainly easier than to the Isles of Scilly. It seemed that living and working on the island would be a dream come true. Sadly, it was not to be. I attended the two-day interview, but felt uncomfortable from the moment that I walked into the school. Apparently, I had interviewed well and got through to the second round of interviews on the following day, with one other person, but the school was not for me. I spent a sleepless night in the hotel near the school and caught the first ferry from the island the following morning back to Southampton, making my excuses with a hasty telephone call to County Hall. I was left in no doubt that my unprofessionalism in pulling out of the interviews would mean that the school would have to repeat the interview process all over again. I suspect that I was banned from the Isle of Wight for many years after that!

My island dream seemed to be on hold. We still visited islands during our summer holidays, as well as venturing to islands such as Majorca and Ibiza, which we enjoyed. However, none had that magical quality that I had experienced on Brownsea Island, Capri, and indeed, the Orkneys.

It was one hastily planned visit to the Canary Islands, when we found ourselves staying on the island of Gran Canaria that I felt for the first time that I had come home, and that my search was over. I still remember that tingling feeling of excitement as we explored so much of the island in such a short space of time. I remember my partner pushing me up the steps of the plane returning home, as I did not want to leave the island. We returned to the island again just a few weeks later, and over the subsequent years, we visited the island many times.

Some years later, when for health reasons, we decided to move to the sun, we both wanted to move to Gran Canaria. However, during that period, as is the case nowadays, getting a job on the island would have been close to impossible. We therefore decided to move to the Costa Blanca where we spent two very happy years. However, it was during that time we both found work with an English language newspaper, and we were asked by the company that we worked for to launch and manage a new English language newspaper in the Canary Islands. Surprisingly, we were to move to the island of Gran Canaria, which is now our Island in the Sun.

Looking Local

Just Call Me Scruffy

Since I seem to have spent most of my working life in a suit, I listened to a recent news item with some amusement. In the Spanish town of Zaragoza, it seems that the local judges have reached the end of their tether about the dress code of the local police. In their frustration, the judges have requested that the police improve their personal cleanliness and appearance, cover their tattoos and stop wearing earrings when on duty, because they are finding it difficult to identify which are the criminals and which are the police during court proceedings.

Needless to say, this seemingly simple request has brought forth a flurry of anger from police officers, and their union. A memo requesting that police officers present themselves in a properly groomed and dressed manner, with a jacket and tie, if possible, seems to have provoked an outrage. Officers make the point that it is easy to identify police officers from criminals, since it is the police officers who are wearing an official badge. Maybe they have missed the point on this one?

The police union has responded by demanding a meeting with the provincial commissioner to request that the memo "be rectified", but admitted that the "communications breakdown" may simply be because the commissioner is new at his job.

Now, don't get me wrong, I'm all for a bit of individuality and quirkiness, when appropriate. The key for me here is 'when appropriate', since I am not a great lover of seeing a bank clerk wearing shorts, tee shirt, chewing gum and with arms covered in tattoos. However, it may be perfectly appropriate for popping down to the beach or off to a club for the evening. Similarly, I would not have the greatest of confidence in a surgeon who is about to operate on me, sporting a ring through his nose or other visible piercings and grotesque tattoos.

I accept that much depends upon the climate. In my example of the bank cashier it would not, for instance, be appropriate for a banker to wear a three piece suit during August in the Canarian climate or, indeed, during any part of the year. Call me old fashioned if you like, but I rather like to see people dressing appropriately for their work, and judging from the Zaragoza example, it seems that I am not the only one with this point of view.

I much prefer to see a nurse in a nice smart, starched uniform, wearing one of those crisp little hats that used to be so popular; a little like those worn by Barbara Windsor in the Carry on Nurse film, I guess. It makes the patient feel so much better without even needing any treatment. Sadly, my last experience in hospital was quite unnerving since a very nice, but unshaven young man in a green smock appeared, who I thought was the cleaner, to tell me that he was my anaesthetist. Before I could complain, he had stuck a needle in my arm, which was probably just as well…

Wearing a Dress to Make a Point

The Canarian Island of Gran Canaria is well known for its 'live and let live' attitude to life, which is one of the reasons why I love this island so much. Whether you are straight, gay, bisexual, transgendered, or just plain confused, it really doesn't matter. If you happen to want to wear a dress instead of trousers few folk will raise as much as an eyebrow, although you would be well advised to have a decent hair do and a full facial to go with it.

Gran Canaria is not adverse to a little cross dressing from time to time, and the right to be flexible when wearing clothing is firmly defended by most generous thinking people on the island. However, a campaign by the taxi divers in our capital city of Las Palmas did raise a few eyebrows recently.

Sadly, the taxi drivers in Las Palmas have been a little upset, because of the policies and demands of the City authorities. They were also more than a little peeved at being asked to wear smart uniforms, which the city authorities felt would improve their presentation when greeting tourists arriving at the airport. A number of other issues also meant that the taxi drivers felt that their work was not valued and that the authorities were undermining them. Anger built up and the taxi drivers felt that the only way that they could protest was not to strike, work to rule, or go on a protest march, but for the male taxi drivers to start wearing dresses, or a skirt and blouse.

Initially, the protesting taxi drivers announced that they would cross dress on Mondays and Wednesdays, leaving the rest of the week for them to recover, as well as giving them the opportunity to refresh their wardrobes, or return items borrowed from wives and girlfriends.

Feelings ran very high, since the taxi drivers felt that this was the only way that would command the attention of the City authorities, as well as a, hopefully, sympathetic public. Many drivers commented that they thought there were far more serious issues to be concerned about than wearing uniforms, as demanded by the City authorities. Indeed, the drivers felt that the area manager, whose Spanish name interestingly translates into 'Mr Tasty', should resign in favour of someone who could resolve the drivers' many grievances.

The president of the taxi drivers' association, who is a woman, commented that she was very proud of her members' actions, as it had started a street movement. In any case, as all holidaymakers to these islands are acutely aware, wearing a skirt is much more comfortable in the Canarian climate than trousers. Don't knock it until you've tried it, seemed to be the general view of these latest cross dressers.

So there we have it. Be warned that if your taxi driver is a friendly, but macho, hairy Canarian sporting a moustache and beard and a broad grin, but also wearing one of the latest frilly numbers from Zara, please don't panic. Just smile and tell him where you wish to go in the usual manner. Please also tip generously, because he may well be saving up for an extension to his wardrobe.

No More 'Tossers' in Tossa del Mar

A recent news item about seven British police officers who were arrested for "brawling" during a stag weekend in Vilnius, Lithuania caught my eye this week. Photographs were published on the social networks showing the officers stumbling and bloodied as they were arrested, handcuffed and dispatched to the local police station.

I suspect that many readers' views on stag and hen parties will rest upon two things; firstly upon their age, and secondly whether or not they have been invited to one recently. Personally, I am open-minded about the whole thing. On the face of it, having a really good night out to celebrate the last days of 'freedom' before getting 'hitched' seems like a good idea. Whilst I have experienced a few stag parties on various levels of disorder in the past, I really have no experience of what 'hens' really do get up to, but I can guess. However, encouraging the prospective bridegroom, in an orgy of male bonding, to become completely comatose on cheap booze before shaving his nether regions and putting him on the overnight ferry to Rotterdam does seem a little unkind, and particularly when the wedding had to be postponed because of his late arrival at church two days later with a broken arm. No, this sad tale really did happen to a friend of ours a few years ago, and the eventual marriage is still recovering from this very shaky start.

"We're having no more it," the good people of Tossa del Mar, in Spain's Costa Brava, have declared. This town has suffered so much from the 'fun' of thoughtless partygoers that they have declared itself to be a 'stag and hen free zone', requiring would be partygoers to apply for a licence, which will never actually be granted because of traditional Spanish bureaucracy, as well as imposing strict fines if revellers are having too much fun. Sadly, this mainly British cultural tradition also seems to be unpopular in Barcelona, Vilnius, Prague… and Bournemouth. Yes, this traditional seaside town of the elderly and language students also has had more than enough, and has recently announced that it is demolishing some of its more popular 'stag and hen' hotels to make way for more classy tourists.

Psychologically speaking, and if I switch off basic common sense for a moment, I can understand the need for a final 'blow out', literally speaking, before the constraints of marriage sets in. It can be an opportunity for a great time with friends, and is a wonderful contrast to the formal set piece performance of meringue dresses and penguin suits that adorns the average wedding. However, maybe now is the time to consider international relations, particularly since the UK seems to have far fewer friends nowadays.

I recall visiting Prague a couple of years ago. We checked into a hotel that we had visited a few years earlier and where we remember being made very welcome. This time, the atmosphere was much cooler and it was over a drink later in the evening when I asked the duty manager, whom I remembered from the previous visit, what had changed. He made it clear that he no longer liked or welcomed British tourists to the city. His main complaint was the vast numbers of revellers visiting his city at weekends. "They have no interest in beauty or tradition; all they want to do is get drunk and have sex with anyone," he complained. Later that evening, I agreed with him after watching several groups of partygoers vomiting their way through the streets of this beautiful city. The hotel manager certainly had a point, and two days later we fled on a train to Bratislava in Slovakia to escape the partying mobs.

Now, back to the ancient and beautiful town of Tossa del Mar, which quaintly translates into 'coughing by the sea'. As one rather large (British) resident succinctly put it on television, in a broad Yorkshire accent, "They'll be no more 'tossers' in Tossa del Mar'. I could have hugged the lady for her sincerity and passion. I am assuming that by using the word 'tosser' she was using the Spanish verb, tosser, which is Spanish for 'medicine', or 'toss' meaning 'cough', which is my feeble excuse for using a such a doubtful title for this story. Clearly, this Yorkshire lady was taking the lead in her attempts to learn Spanish, as well as considering the health benefits to prospective tourists.

I am sure that most stag and hen parties are great fun, but since the participants are clearly not interested in historical sites, museums or fine wines and local food, maybe I could suggest a couple of nights in Blackpool or Skegness instead? After a few pints, it would feel more or less the same, but would be much cheaper and not cause such a strain on international relations. Maybe the British police officers arrested in Lithuania could bear this in mind next time?

Sunshine, Cactus and Roses

I had an interesting email from Joyce, a newly arrived expat, this week. Although I am often asked about issues relating to living and working in Spain and the Canary Islands, this question was unusual in that it asked me about gardening. Joyce and her partner have just moved to the Canary Islands and were wondering what she could grow in the small, but much appreciated, garden at the front of her new home. Joyce was a keen gardener in the UK, yet was now concerned, because she didn't just want to grow cactus, which she thought were the only plants that would grow in the desert-like conditions of the south of Gran Canaria.

I am no gardening expert, other than I know what I like and what I don't like. As with most things, I am a firm believer that most problems can be resolved with the aid of a good book, and in this case a good gardening book, a soil test kit, a lot of patience and a bit of common sense should do the trick. The more I thought about the question, the more I realised that I have learned quite a lot about gardening and plants whilst living on this lovely island. Admittedly, I have made many mistakes, with the most common being trying to grow plants that I liked when I lived in the UK. Of course, the plants did not share the same point of view and would have none of it, and quickly shrivelled and died. A combination of soil type, lively winds, dusty dry heat and lack of water were the reasons for many of my failures, and so I began to look for plants that I could see growing in other gardens, which would also be suitable for our own.

Gardening is not as popular a pastime in Spain and the Canary Islands as it is in the UK; I often hear that gardening and the love of plants is a Brit thing. I have also noticed that when Spanish and Canarians move into a new home with a space for a garden, their first reaction is to tile over any remaining ground. Admittedly, it is easier to keep clean, and ornate pots filled with plants can make all the difference. However, as a Brit, I like to see plants growing in the soil, albeit with the aid of a watering system beneath the surface of the soil, with the water supply controlled by a programmable timer to ensure that the plants don't dry out during the very hot, dry days. Our watering system switches on for two minutes, twice a day, during the winter months and for five minutes, twice a day, during the hot, summer months. The periods of hot winds are the worst time for plants, and this is why the choice of plants is so important for any garden.

I avoid prickly cactus, not that I don't like them; I do, and many have beautiful, impressive flowers. However, our dog, Bella, tends to run into them when she is over exited or chasing a ball, and a dog with prickly cactus needles in her bottom is not a good idea. Instead, I aim for lush succulents, and cactus without prickles. They are usually good value to buy and provide an interesting variety of shape and colour. Interestingly, roses also survive beautifully in our garden and they flower throughout the year. Unlike in the UK, I never have to spray them for black spot or any other disease that affects roses in many parts of the UK. I cut them back heavily in January each year and give them a granular feed, and they reward us with a beautiful display of blooms throughout the year. Finding good quality roses to buy is not always easy on the island, but the garden centre that I use imports good stock from time to time, and I try to buy the scented varieties.

I have also found that lavender is a wonderful asset for a Canarian garden. They grow and flower vigorously, require little attention other than cutting back from time to time, and their heady perfume is enough to send flies, mosquitoes and other nasty insects heading in another direction.

My message to Joyce is to enjoy her Canarian garden, but to work with the soil, the plants and local growing conditions. There are plenty of plants that can be grown very successfully, but I would focus upon succulents, roses and lavender. Also, don't forget to plant Aloe Vera, which is often regarded as a weed and ignored. It is commonly known as the 'First Aid Plant', and for good reason. If you should scratch yourself whilst pruning the roses, breaking a piece off this wonderful plant and rubbing it over the wound, provides a soothing remedy that has been known and used by Canarians for generations.

Strawberries, Cheese and the White Bottomed Bumble Bee

There was a serious clash on the islands last week. No, I am not talking about the heat generated from the forthcoming Spanish elections, or squabbling drag queens, but a ferocious clash between two food festivals in the old town of Santa Maria de Guia in the north west of Gran Canaria. The youngest food festival upstart, the Strawberry Festival, suddenly announced that they would hold their festival on the same day as the well-established Cheese Festival, which is its senior by 35 years. Well, you can imagine the shock horror of the townspeople, which I guess would be very similar to the indignation felt by the good ladies of the UK's Women's Institute should the date for an upstart dog show be on the same date as their annual jam making competition. Fur and feathers, if not jam and pickles, would fly. In the strawberries and cheese clash, good old-fashioned Canarian common sense would eventually be applied, with the cheese festival being repeated the following week. Cheese and strawberry lovers could therefore enjoy both. What a beautiful combination too!

The Canary Islands know a thing or two about growing strawberries, with the municipality of Valsequillo being one of the few municipalities on the island of Gran Canaria that doesn't reach the coast. As such, the climate is perfect for growing strawberries, with over one million kilos of strawberries grown each year for local consumption, as well as for export. Well-tried techniques are used to improve the quality and quantity of the crop, including setting garlic plants around the strawberry plants to ward off various insects that could damage the ripening fruit. White bottomed bumblebees are also recruited to pollinate the flowers on the strawberry fields, but please don't ask me how the bumblebees came to have white bottoms. The result of all this hard work from Canarian farmers, together with a little help from garlic and white bottomed bumble bees is delicious sweet tasting fruit, the like of which I have not tasted since growing up in rural Lincolnshire, and eating strawberries from the family garden.

As much as I enjoy eating strawberries throughout the year, my mind sometimes goes back to those childhood days when strawberries were only available for a few weeks of each year. How I used to look forward to those summer tea times when, I suspect, I enjoyed them even more due to their seasonal scarcity. Maybe, in some ways, the ease of being able to buy strawberries, raspberries and what used to be other delicacies out of their normal growing season has taken the edge off the enjoyment felt when we knew that we could only enjoy them for a few precious weeks.

As far as possible, we only purchase strawberries grown in Valsequillo, or other parts of the island. Sometimes, stocks are low and we are reduced to purchasing fruit from the local supermarket that has been imported from mainland Spain. The punnets of fruit look delicious enough with huge, red juicy fruit that is tempting to the eye, but are nearly always disappointing. Just one bite into the pallid, tasteless, watery flesh always makes me appreciate the qualities of the genuine Canarian strawberry even more.

A recent news article in a UK newspaper proudly boasted that strawberries are now available for 20 weeks a year, which is seen as a huge advance from just six weeks that was common in the 1990s. Now the UK strawberry season stretches from May to October, with any gaps in supply filled with chilled and often tasteless imports from Morocco, Israel, Jordan and, of course, Spain. I am told that strawberries were seen on the shelves of UK supermarkets as late as December for the first time last year. The secret of the UK growers' success is the increasing use of polytunnels - huge flexible plastic greenhouses that stretch for acres across the British countryside, whereas in the 1990s there were none. Changing climate too has a part to play in the strawberry growers' success with mild winters and record levels of sunlight.

Back to Gran Canaria, and our plentiful supply of sweet, juicy strawberries for most of the year. I am pleased to report that both food festivals were a huge success and that the good people of Santa Maria de Guia can now enjoy both strawberries and cheese without fear of neighbourhood repercussions, and with grateful thanks to the white bottomed bumble bee.

A Bit of a Storm - a reality check

"Gran Canaria in shock after freak thunderstorm" screamed the headlines! Well, it is August and the Daily Hate clearly has little more to report other than a drop of rain and a few bangs and crashes somewhere on a small island in the Atlantic. Are we in shock? I don't think so. Annoyed maybe, since many locals and myself have spent a good part of the morning hosing and washing patios and cars free of the 'red rain' that has found its way here from Algeria. Anyway, what's a couple of centimetres of warm, but muddy rain in the greater scheme of things? This is part of the August 'fun', alongside temperatures sometimes hitting 40 degrees, together with a few calimas bringing sand and dust from the Sahara.

Don't misunderstand me; I am full of sympathy for holidaymakers who have spent their hard earned cash to escape from a wet and cold UK in search of a week or two in the sun. Of course, they will be annoyed, angry and I guess a few other adjectives will be heard, but it really isn't the island's fault, and even in the rain it is still warm. The best thing is to try to ignore it and do what the locals do, frolic in the rain and enjoy it as a delicious rarity, knowing that the sun is taking a bit of a break, but will be back again with a vengeance shortly.

Of course, I blame much of it on Ptolemy, from ancient times, and his comment that the Canary Islands are "The Fortunate Isles". The poor man meant well I guess, and we probably do have the best climate in the world, but the quirks of weather on a tiny piece of land in the Atlantic is quite a different matter. Ptolemy unwittingly gave the impression that everything is glorious all the time. Well, it may come as a surprise to some, but it isn't.

Just ask a local living in Las Palmas about 'the donkey's belly', which hangs over the city for several weeks in the summer, and is the reason why so many of its residents head to the south of the island on their days off, whilst many wealthier families have purchased apartments in the south of the island. Ask residents living in that idyllic resort of Puerto Mogan why they spend much of their time in air-conditioned apartments, shopping centres, hotels and bars during July and August instead of on the beach, and they will tell you it is just too hot to go outside. Ask residents of Pozo Izquierdo how they cope living in a wind tunnel for much of the year? After all, it is the home of the annual wind surfing championships, but is also billed as "the windiest place on the planet".

Residents living in the quaint mountain villages and towns in the north and west of the island can be heard complaining about the endless rain and cold that they have endured this year; sales of heating appliances have sky rocketed. Unlike the UK, most homes here do not have wall-to-wall carpets, central heating, damp proof courses, guttering or even a simple door threshold to keep out the rain. Rising damp, mould and flooding can be a problem following a heavy storm for many homes on the island.

Despite some of the problems that I have described, many still regard living on these islands as being as close to paradise as we can get. However, let us not be blinded to "the fortunate isles" being so idyllic that we ignore the reality of changing weather patterns and the quirks of the Atlantic. A little variety is good for us, just as long as we don't chase around too much, roast on the beach, or go mountain trekking in 40 degrees.

Are we in shock after the freak thunderstorm? Of course not. Many of us have welcomed it as bringing freshness into the air, settling dust in dry areas, refreshing plants and bringing some greenness and new life back to arid land for a short time. It's all positively fun-filled. Anyway, the sun is out again now and it will probably be a couple of months before we see any more rain.

Back to the Daily Hate and similar publications. If there is no news, please don't make it up. I often long for a day when the newspaper is published with just one simple headline - "No news today"! Now that would be well worth paying for, although I guess they would quickly go out of business.

112 - Emergency, Emergency!

Do you know how to contact emergency services, such as asking for medical assistance, ambulance, police or fire services? If you are in the UK, most people will know that when you dial 999 you will receive prompt and efficient attention to whatever crisis that you find yourself in. What about when you are overseas on holiday, or maybe living in another country as an expat?

I was surprised to learn that there are many holidaymakers and expats living in Spain, the Canary Islands and other parts of Europe who not know how to contact the relevant emergency services. Services equivalent to the UK's 999 service exist in all European countries, which can be easily accessed by dialling 112.

In Spain and the Canary Islands, for instance, assistance is offered in English, Spanish, German, Italian and French, so there is no need to worry about language barriers. This 112 Emergency Service is available to everyone 24 hours a day, and for 365 days a year, free of charge from any fixed telephone line or mobile, and without the need for any dialling codes.

Recently, I visited one of the two 112 coordinating centres for the Canary Islands in Las Palmas de Gran Canaria, which opened in 1998, becoming part of the European System for Emergency Response. This centre is a public service, with similar centres operating in each of Spain's provinces.

In the Canary Islands, many of its emergency services are water-related accidents, such as accidents at sea or at the beaches, as well as the usual range of medical, police and fire incidents.

In the operations room, I saw calls being received, and information being collected by a co-ordinator of services and efficiently categorised before being referred to one of the specialist teams based in the centre. In the case of a health emergency, a doctor on duty at the centre answers the call, assesses the situation before responding with an ambulance, helicopter or plane to deal with the emergency. Security and fire emergencies are dealt with in a similar manner. In addition, the centre is able to give support to women suffering from domestic violence, who are given immediate advice and support.

Of course, this support is a two-way process, so that if you are involved in an incident that requires help from the emergency services, it is important that all the necessary questions are answered correctly. It is vital to give clear and accurate information at this stage in order to receive the best possible support.

For holidaymakers and residents living in the Canary Islands, there is a recent new addition to the service, which is unique to the Canary Islands, and a few other locations. This is a service called FRESS, which is the Next Generation Emergency Response, and is available as a free App that can be downloaded for most mobile phones.

This exciting innovation allows those facing an emergency to simply press a button to activate FRESS on their phone and receive immediate and enhanced support from the 112 response team. FRESS connects by voice, instant text message or video communication, and automatically sends your location, name, age, phone number and previously recorded medical details to the centre, as well as translating the emergency call into the required language.

Although, currently, FRESS is only operating on a trial basis in some areas of Poland, Italy, the US, Mexico, the Philippines and Malaysia, it is now fully operational in the Canary Islands, which has provided an ideal location for such a service to be thoroughly tested. It was fascinating to learn of the possibilities that this life saving app could give. It has the potential to operate worldwide, doing away with the need to remember a whole host of emergency numbers that other countries use, such as 999, 112, 911 and 066. As it develops, FRESS will offer huge safety benefits to travellers, holidaymakers and expats worldwide.

I was impressed to witness the skills, dedication and support given by the team on duty during my visit. It is a service that I guess we rarely think about until we need it. For holidaymakers and expats, it is important to remember that support is given in five languages, including English. It is good to know that it is there for us all in an emergency.

Getting Political

Expats are Migrants Too

From the time that we moved to the Canary Islands, each year has brought with it attempts by migrants to land on the islands. Some attempts have been successful, whilst the police, as well as Frontex, the European organisation charged with tracking and dissuading migrants from arriving in Spain and other European countries, have thwarted others. Most migrants are from sub Saharan Africa, in search of a better life and prospects in Europe. The arrival of migrants reached a peak of 32,000 in 2006, but fell to around 300 in 2014, which was mainly due to increased patrolling and effective border controls.

Since that time, the issue has become much more serious in Europe, and the occasional flow of mostly economic migrants from African countries has turned into a massive exodus of refugees from Syria, Iraq, Afghanistan, as well as from several African countries, including Mauritania and Senegal. In most cases, we are no longer talking about economic migrants, but refugees in fear of their lives, sufficiently desperate to take enormous risks for themselves and their families in order to start a new life in a country where they feel safe.

A few days ago, the situation worsened, when a boat holding 40 migrants from Africa, including a baby girl, arrived on a beach in Gran Canaria. They were discovered huddled together on the beach in darkness, and Red Cross volunteers gave them blankets and water. This incident in Gran Canaria is just a tiny example of what has been happening on the

Syrian/Turkish border, Italy, Greece, Hungary and Calais; desperate people looking for safety.

In recent days, I have been horrified to read some of the negative, cruel and thoughtless comments about refugees on social media, and particularly from a number of expats living in Spain and the Canary Islands, who should know better. Some have seen it as nothing more than a potential irritating interference in the usually smooth pattern of their daily lives, as well as angry comments from potential visitors concerned that an influx of refugees could disturb their holiday plans on our sunshine islands. Others have seen a boat full of exhausted men, women and children as nothing more than an inconvenient drain upon the islands' health and welfare resources.

What has happened to love and basic humanity? I know that many of the comments that I have read stem from fear and ignorance of the plight of so many desperate people. Fear always comes from the unknown and, has history has shown, is at the root of xenophobia and terrible acts of cruelty that were common during the two World Wars. People under threat always blame minority groups; those with a different religion, different colour of skin or different values. This fear contributes to prejudice and hate, which often leads to terrible consequences.

What many expats voicing fear and hatred demonstrate, although they have every right to express their opinions, is complete ignorance of the fact that they too, as expats, are migrants. It is true that our circumstances are very different, but many of those who criticise fail to see the irony of their comments. Thanks to the European Union, many of us have chosen to live and work in another country; we have not been forced to flee by oppressive regimes, butchering militants, or dictators to seek a new life in the sun. Most of us could afford a plane or boat ticket to get us to our destination; we have passports and identity papers that demonstrate our right to live anywhere in Europe. We do not have to fall into the hands of people smugglers, taking the little money that we have to be crowded onto small, unseaworthy boats, suffocating vans and lorries to risk our lives trying to reach safety. Most of us were fortunate enough to be able to rent or buy a home, stay with friends, or at least have a roof over our heads and a bed to sleep in; not cowering on a dark beach at night relying upon charity and strangers speaking in a language that we don't understand.

It is purely an accident of birth that we did not find ourselves in the same situation as these refugees; born in another country or continent and in the hands of tyrants. As expats, we need to remember that we are migrants too. Now is time that we should show love, compassion and understanding, as well as insisting upon practical support for the vulnerable refugees from those who lead us.

The Solidarity Fridge

As a child, I was a fussy eater and vividly remember leaving food on my plate, which would always lead to an abrupt ticking off from my mother. She would inevitably add the comment, "Barrie, if you don't eat it, I will send it to the poor, starving children in Africa who would be glad of it." As annoying as it was at the time, I still remember my mother's words and I am grateful for them; as a result, I hate to see food wasted and thrown away.

The World recession has brought into sharp focus the appalling poverty and helpless situation that many people find themselves in, and which many governments are unwilling or unable to rectify. In the UK and many parts of Europe, the lack of basic essentials, such as a warm home, food and clothing are denied to many, and are a sad reflection of a so-called civilised society. In the UK, child poverty and homelessness remain at disgracefully high levels for one of the wealthiest countries in the world.

In Spain and the Canary Islands, food banks have become part of the pattern of existence for many people, and it is now a common sight for charity collections of basic food items to be collected from wealthier shoppers during their weekly visit to the supermarket. On this small holiday island, it is a sad reflection of our times that charity food collections are taking place just a few yards from some of the country's most expensive and luxurious hotels; where wealthy holidaymakers enjoy sumptuous quantities of food and five star accommodation.

I was very interested to hear of a recent development to help the poor and needy by the installation of a 'Solidarity Fridge' in one of Spain's cities. The 'Solidarity Fridge' is a large white refrigerator that has been installed in a prominent position on the pavement in the small city of Galdakao, which is near Bilbao. A fence surrounds the fridge to tell people that it is not just an abandoned appliance, but a pioneering project aimed at reducing food wastage. Restaurants and residents are encouraged to place leftover or unused food, which would otherwise be put into a bin, into the fridge and made available to those in need. Any item that is left in the fridge can be taken by anyone, and particularly those in need.

There are strict rules in place preventing donors from leaving raw fish, meat, eggs, canned or packaged goods that are past their use by date. Any home cooked food must include a label about when it was made. A typical day might see unopened milk cartons, sandwiches or a left over casserole left in the fridge.

This idea came from realising how much edible food local supermarkets were throwing out. Local research led to discovering a similar successful scheme in Berlin, which operates a network of shared fridges. The Spanish city realised that they could make it work for their city too, and so a small group of volunteers was established to make it happen, as well as obtaining agreement, licencing and support from the city authorities.

As well as making food available to those in need, the

aim of the Solidarity Fridge is to make use of food that would otherwise end up in the bin. Anyone is allowed to take food from the fridge, as and when they need it. Volunteers keep an eye on the contents of the fridge, removing out of date items and the organisers report that so far all of the food has been taken each day that the fridge has been in use.

For some with sensitive and well-honed palettes, the idea of collecting and eating food discarded by others may sound distasteful. However, for those in need, wondering where their next meal is coming from, the idea must seem heaven sent. In addition, reducing food wastage in a world where there is widespread hunger and starvation must be welcome. The idea of a 'Solidarity Fridge' has now spread to a second Spanish city, Murcia, and enquiries are being received from all over the country, as well as other countries interested in starting similar schemes. It just goes to show that the seeds of one thoughtful, simple idea can quickly spread for the benefit of others.

Keeping the Vote

I recently received an email from a fellow blogger, urging me to encourage all expats who read my blogs to vote in the next UK General Election. Apparently, only 30,000 of the 2.5 million expats who have the right to vote, bother to do so. This is where the interesting politics begins since one of the UK political parties, currently in Government, is getting a tad concerned that it may be voted out of office in the 2015 General Election. This is where the sudden interest in the expat vote begins.

For those who are unaware, British expats have the right to vote in a UK General Election under the 15-year rule, meaning that after 15 years we lose the right to vote. My fellow blogger went on to say that because she had lived outside the UK for the last 25 years she was unhappy that she no longer had the right to vote in the UK. The email duly instructed me to support a host of Conservative MPs in support of their campaigns, as well as ensuring that I vote Conservative to ensure that this political party fulfils their promise to ensure that the voting rights for all expats are permanently extended.

I have several problems with this proposal. Firstly, I am not about to suddenly become a supporter of the UK's Conservative Party, nor to follow the dictates of their Chairman who came up with this brilliant wheeze to garner more support for a party that was likely to lose the next General Election. My cynicism comes from the belief that if the party had really wanted to do this they could have done so during their present and previous periods in Government, when the expat voice was conveniently ignored. How times change.

Secondly, I am no longer interested in voting in UK elections. Don't get me wrong, I love the UK and always will, but as I have been out of the country for the last twelve years, I no longer feel that I have the right to vote. Each time I return to the country, I feel that I no longer belong. I fail to understand the surge in support for parties such as UKIP, the SNP and the recent near debacle in Scotland. Frankly, I am much more interested in being able to vote in the Spanish General Election as this will directly affect me. As a Spanish resident I can already vote in European and local elections, but cannot currently vote in the national elections of the country where I live, work and pay taxes. This, to me, seems more unjust than not being able to vote in the country of my birth.

No doubt many will disagree with me and I can see their point of view, particularly if they intend to return to the UK in the future, have families in the UK, pay UK taxes and receive UK pensions. If this should be the case, they can apply for a vote in the UK by registering for a postal vote on: https://www.gov.uk/register-to-vote. I am told that the procedure is simple and it will take only three minutes to make the Chairman of the Conservative Party a very happy person. On second thoughts, maybe I will apply for a vote, but maybe not use it as intended…

The Scourge of Meetings

I am not a great lover of meetings - any meetings. I am sure that this comes from my days as a teacher when endless staff meetings were the order of the day. I remember hours spent discussing sports days, Christmas parties and the colour of paint for classrooms, when I would much rather have been marking pupils' books and planning lessons for the next busy day. This is not to say that sports days and Christmas parties were unimportant, they were, but most issues could have been dealt with efficiently in minutes rather than the three hours often wasted after a busy school day, when most good teachers are exhausted.

It was after reading an article in an American management journal, hastily written for the American 'How to be a manager in three easy lessons' market, that I picked up a valuable nugget of advice that was to guide my future views and actions towards meetings. The theory was that no meeting should last for more than one hour; after all, anything that couldn't be dealt with within one hour was not important enough to discuss anyway. It was true, and I resolved that in my future career as a head teacher, and later as a school inspector, I would follow this guidance whenever possible.

This resolute approach to chairing meetings, not surprisingly, met with some initial resistance. The usual practice of staff drifting in late to meetings, making a cup of coffee, chatting about the day, and complaining about parents and children had to come to an abrupt end. After all, discussions of this kind could continue after our meeting, but never before. My colleagues quickly learned to focus upon a pre-prepared and manageable agenda, which allowed for succinct discussion and to focus upon only what was important. Meetings took place under a strict one-hour rule, agenda items were routinely and efficiently dealt with, leaving time to focus upon what was really important, teaching and learning, as well as going home at a reasonable time. Endless discussions about Christmas parties and sports days became a thing of the past.

All this had to come to an abrupt end when I moved to Spain, where community meetings take place to deal with issues that may affect the residents of an apartment block or community area. In theory, it is a good and democratic idea, but once again, I was faced with endless meetings called to resolve such issues as lifts not working, the electric door to the communal garage not opening, and the eccentricity of the electricity supply. Meetings scheduled to start at 7.30pm eventually began at 8.30pm, with participants coming and going, babies crying, as well as texting and answering mobile phones during the meeting. The lack of an agenda, and roaming from one subject to another, as well as the whole procedure taking place in machine gun Spanish, meant that I eventually left the meetings, four hours later, exhausted, bewildered and very angry.

Last night we attended a village meeting to discuss a number of issues. We felt it was important to show solidarity and to share concern about the issues to be discussed; after all, such meetings are an important part of local democracy. Eventually, the meeting started; there were several angry monologues from local worthies, together with many interruptions and much shouting from a number of residents. After one hour we slipped away quietly to the bar next door to enjoy a pizza and a few drinks, whilst the meeting continued into the early hours of the morning. I am so pleased that I read that article in the American management journal; it has given me many hours of my life back.

Let Them Eat Gold!

Christmas and the New Year holiday season is a time of year when the stark contrast between those who have and those who have not pricks the conscience of most of us, if only fleetingly. It may be the homeless man on the street, or the woman outside the supermarket begging for coins to buy food to feed her children that draws our attention to the poverty and plight of many people around us. These are not people living in some far off continent, but real people who live, and try to survive in our own communities. In the Canary Islands, Spain and the UK, food banks may be the only and last refuge for the needy and desperate. Most of us are fortunate in having enough to survive; it may not be great wealth, but hopefully we can feed ourselves, our families, and have a roof over our heads.

Unemployment in the Canary Islands and Spain remains horrifically high, and is particularly shocking for the lost generation of young people who have been worst hit by the world's financial crisis. No civilised society should tolerate such a waste of energy, enthusiasm and talent as we are currently seeing in relatively wealthy European countries, but it seems that the rich and powerful are unable or unwilling to do anything significant to change it. In the UK and Spain we often hear about the "ongoing years of austerity", which leaves many to question whether austerity is a desirable state of affairs from the point of view of the political elite. Is it designed to keep the working classes in their place, profits high and wages low to benefit those in power, as well as those who are better educated or just fortunate?

The Canarian village that I live in is not a wealthy one. Many of its residents are unemployed, or have just one member of the household bringing in a low wage; that is if they are fortunate. Working hours are long and working conditions are mostly poor in a range of activities from hotel catering, fishing and seasonal agriculture. Even so, the villagers recognise that there are many within their community who have very little to survive on and they organised a 'Solidarity Gala' to support the needy during the festive season. The price of entry? No cash, because there is very little to spare; the entry fee was just one kilogram of unopened food.

I contrast this heart warming attempt to do something positive about real poverty in a community, to a sickening account of a bakery in Andalusia, Spain, that is baking loaves of bread cooked with gold dust, which is being sold for 117 euros for each loaf to the rich, wealthy or powerful. It is being promoted as the 'world's most expensive', with loaves selling like 'hot cakes' to Arab, Russian and Chinese buyers. Each 400 gram loaf of bread contains whole wheat dough and dehydrated honey. It addition, it contains one additional ingredient: 250 milligrams of gold dust, allegedly worth 100 euros. As well as receiving considerable interest from foreign buyers, a national supermarket chain is also showing interest in stocking and selling the product.

I guess that the same could be said about expensive watches, mobile phones, perfumes and cars, and I may be lacking a sense of humour and realism this festive season. However, I find the 'upgrade' and sale of such a basic and essential product as bread to be a callous disregard of the poverty and hunger that surrounds us. There should be no need for food banks, since there is more than enough food for everyone to share if we reduce our own consumption and greed, and curb such frivolous, pointless nonsense, such as eating gold. For many families in the world, a decent loaf of bread would be more than enough to satisfy them for a day or two. Now, where did I read that eating gold is actually toxic to the human system?

Oil Slicks, Turtles and Lies

During the last week or so, one major news story has hit the headlines and dominated the airwaves in the Canary Islands. It has led to fiery exchanges between politicians and environmentalists, with some evidence that a 'massaged' account of events was being released to the press from those who have a heavy investment in the tourist industry. Thankfully, there were others, including the environmental group, Greenpeace, who rapidly assessed the situation and gave a more balanced account of the crisis that is currently hitting the shores of these islands.

A Russian trawler, the Oleg Naydenov, which was often denounced by Greenpeace for illegal fishing activities, caught fire in the port of Las Palmas, Gran Canaria. The vessel was carrying 1,500 tonnes of fuel oil, and the port authorities decided to tow it out to sea, about 15 nautical miles south of Gran Canaria, to let it sink and, presumably, to forget about it.

The trawler is currently leaking between five and 10 litres of fuel oil an hour into open sea, and a robot submarine has detected that the wreckage is now located over two miles below sea level. Both the Spanish and Canarian governments are looking at plans to either remove the remainder of the oil from the sunken vessel, or seal the holes in the hull that are causing the leak; both will be difficult and expensive operations.

Despite initial government denials about the severity of the problem and a less than frank account at a news conference, oil slicks were spotted on Greenpeace satellite images off the coast of the south of Gran Canaria, with oil appearing on several beaches. Interestingly, the government has, so far, refused to release satellite images of the area for the public to see. As well as a being a major tourist area, the seas around the Canary Islands are rich in marine and bird life and already birds, turtles, as well an endangered loggerhead sea turtle have been found covered in oil.

Greenpeace are currently monitoring the situation, and warn that the contamination could worsen in the coming days. With an eye on the tourist industry, government officials continue to play down the crisis. However, none of the beaches affected have been closed to visitors; indeed, I visited one yesterday and there was no sign of any pollution, although locals told me that council staff and volunteers had been there earlier in the day to clear away a small amount of oil.

Hindsight is a wonderful thing, but it seems that the government's decision to tow the fire stricken, fuel laden Russian fishing boat into open sea and let it sink may not have been the cleverest, or most environmentally friendly decision it could have made. In their defence, government sources claim that the decision to tow the trawler out to sea was to avoid the burning vessel contaminating the water desalination plant nearby. The Spanish government has now announced an enquiry into the issue, and to consider what could have been done to avoid the catastrophe.

Many are comparing the current issues with the oil spill from the Prestige oil tanker in 2002, when 60,000 tonnes of oil poured into the sea off northern

Spain. A few months ago, many islanders were concerned about the exploration for oil and gas that was taking place off the Canary Islands. Fortunately, the findings were of insufficient quality or quantity to develop commercially; the price of oil fell and the project was terminated, at least for the time being. Although the current spill is minor in comparison to the Prestige oil tanker disaster, it does serve as a warning of what could happen should, one day, oil exploration and extraction resume off the coast of these beautiful, and environmentally rich islands.

Joining In

The Canary Islander

That Eurovision Feeling

It's that time of the year again; time for the annual Eurovision Song Contest when Eurosceptics and Eurovision haters band together to pour sneering snobbery and scorn upon the UK's song entry, whatever it may be. Listening to the Eurovision haters is actually great fun, particularly since they are truly passionate in their hatred of the song, and the performers, regardless of talent that they may have. Such critics tend to forget that the Eurovision Song Content will capture the attention of citizens of many nations for one enjoyable evening in May. They will add into their argument comments, such as, "We won't win anyway, we never do", or "It's a stitch up", and even "It's nothing like Sandie Shaw", with the supposed killer comment being, "It's all based on politics". Well really? Now, that's a surprise! Didn't their teachers ever tell them that it's not winning, but the taking part that is important?

The Eurovision Song Contest is, in many ways, rather like Blackpool, Benidorm and Marmite; you either love them or hate them. In my case, I love them all, and particularly Eurovision, which I have watched and enjoyed since childhood. This annual extravaganza taught me a lot about geography, since I would check out the countries represented in the contest in my atlas, and the people and languages represented would always fascinate me. Maybe it also set the seeds of curiosity that eventually led me to live a life outside the UK. Of course, I still remember that old trouper, Katie Boyle, a personification of BBC professionalism, as she would make contact with the faceless juries in Rome, Madrid and Paris, whilst dreading those awful words, "nil point".

I value the cooperation and friendship that Eurovision stands for. It is refreshing to hear Europeans discussing songs instead of the usual arguments and debates about budgets and unemployment. My usual response to the Eurovision cynics is "If you don't like it, don't listen to it". They seem to miss the point that it is not to be taken too seriously. It is just an evening of cheesy fun, high camp, glitz, and catchy showcase spectaculars. It is rarely about the quality of a song and its music. How could it be with so many countries and languages and cultures represented, and does it matter anyway?

If I go into a German, Scandinavian, Irish or Spanish bar and ask "Who likes the Eurovision Song Contest?" the overwhelming response will be positive. If I tried that in a British bar, I guess I would be booed and laughed out of the premises. Yet come the big day, Brits will also head off to bars and parties to watch the event on the big screens, as will their European counterparts. It is almost as if Brits are afraid or unwilling to applaud anything that is remotely European, or maybe being seen to enjoy it.

In many ways, the Eurovision Song Contest represents British suspicion of Europe and its institutions. The dislike and distrust of Europe that is now gaining ground in the UK is the result of entrenched insular attitudes of many of its citizens; flames fanned by immigration issues, unemployment and a range of other social issues, which are now finding a political voice. Sadly, I guess that the UK will never be a true and willing partner that is comfortable within Europe and sharing the European dream; negative attitudes towards Eurovision reflect many of these issues.

I am delighted that Australia is taking part in the contest this year. I have many Australian friends who are great fans of the contest, and it is my hope that Aussie enthusiasm and their usual pragmatism will help to lighten some of the more cynical British attitudes. I will be watching the contest, supporting both the UK and Spain, although I am not that bothered who wins the contest. However, I do know that it will be a good evening spent with friends from a range of countries. Personally, I would love to see a Worldwide Song Contest, which would be a refreshing change from viewing the world through the barrel of a gun.

Playing the Game

One of the many benefits of living in the Canary Islands is that, as residents, we are entitled to half price travel to the other islands, as well as to the Spanish Peninsular. It is a discount well worth having but, as many residents will already know, the rules keep changing. It's not just a simple matter of a one off application for a certificate to be presented to the airline or shipping company, but a repeated six month document renewal process, where one appears at the Town Hall, presents assorted documents, which vary according to the month and mood of the officiating clerk, and payment of a small fee. If we are fortunate, we escape within an hour or so clutching the precious piece of paper that will give us a healthy discount off our travel costs. On the other hand, we could be there for most of the morning, which is why taking a chair, water and a packet of sandwiches is always highly recommended.

In theory of course, all that should be necessary is to enter our National Identity numbers when we make the booking with the airline, which the system should automatically check against the register of residents for a particular municipality. Of course, life is never quite that simple and I still recall a nasty incident at the airport, which resulted in a panic taxi ride from the airport back to my home to collect the precious document, despite the system having confirmed my discount entitlement, and returning to the airport with just minutes to spare before the flight took off. Needless to say, I was not amused, and it was particularly hurtful when the offending clerk could not be bothered to give the document even a cursory look; she just gave me a smirk as I headed through check in. It was just one of those games that are played over here, and on this occasion I had not played the game very well. This incident confirms my long-standing view that nothing is ever quite as it seems, and we sometimes unwittingly pop into an 'Alice in Wonderland' situation with no hope of escape. Just play the game.

Of course, some readers will be thinking, "Why doesn't he do it online?" Yes, again, that is possible, in theory, but victims still have to attend the Town Hall to pay the fee. Payment on line? Just forget it and play the game.

This time, the counter clerk required a photocopy of the residency document before she would proceed. I didn't like to point out that they already had all the information required on their systems, since we have been doing the same thing for the last umpteen years. I asked if I could get a copy of the document in the building. The clerk grimaced, pointing to the security guard. "He'll get one for you, if he feels like it," she growled.

The security guard seemed to be a very nice man, who actually smiled and nodded, made a small charge before he disappeared upstairs with our residency documents. Experience has taught me that the Spanish love nothing more that reams of paper, and if any important-looking paper is offered to them it is immediately grabbed, whether it is useful or not, and rarely ever seen again. Incidentally, this is the one piece of essential, possibly life saving advice that I give to all would be expats. Never, ever hand over an original document, unless you make several copies first. It is a game of chance that is often played with the newly arrived and over-enthusiastic expat. You will never win; so just accept that once you hand over an original document it is gobbled up into the Spanish bureaucratic system, and that is the last that you will ever see of it. Fortunately, there are very rare exceptions, and on this occasion, the very nice security guard reappeared clutching two crisp photocopies, as well as willingly returning the original documents. This must be a first!

Once we had the photocopies, we queued at the cash machine for a ticket. Panic set in when we realised that we had only three euros and we needed four and that the machine would not accept the new ten euro notes. Fortunately, I also had a twenty euro note and unwilling as I am to plunge notes into machines, this one had the good grace to accept the note, before eventually spewing out two receipts, as well as the correct change. Maybe, just maybe I was winning this particular game. We made our way back to the lady at the issuing desk, who actually smiled and told us that she would be with us in a moment. A smile and a polite greeting at the Town Hall? Now that is a pleasant surprise.

The next part of the story may sound politically incorrect, as well as sexist, but I really do not care. I have often maintained that women are far better at multi tasking than men; if you want a job doing well, be it decorating or rodding the drains, possibly at the same time, then get a good woman to do the job. What follows next is a perfect example of what I mean.

The smiling lady called us over to her counter. She examined our receipts and attempted to staple them to the precious travel documents. Sadly, the stapler had run out of staples, which is why she performed her party trick. With her right hand she opened the stapler, retrieved a new strip of staples from a packet in her drawer, inserted them into the stapler, stapled both documents at the same time as she was bonking another client's documents with her left hand, as well as answering their questions. In addition, she answered a telephone call with the receiver trapped somewhere between her neck, ample bosoms and shoulder blade. It was a truly impressive sight that left me speechless. I really should have given her a round of applause, but I restrained myself and we left clutching the precious pieces of paper. A visit to the Town Hall is always so exciting, just as long as we play the game.

Kisses, Cuddles and Coffee

Banks have not had a good press in recent years, and their misdeeds have caught up with many of these seemingly impervious institutions, both in the UK, as well as in Spain. On a local level, I read a rather sad news item last week about a bank manager working in a small town in Gran Canaria who was caught fiddling the books and extracted around 15,000 euros from other people's accounts. Fortunately, he was caught before he inflicted too much damage on more of his customers and the bank, but it serves to remind us all that there are rotten apples in all walks of life and in all countries.

This news story coincided with another article that I read, written by a British expat living in Spain. The subject was banking in Spain, and it made me wonder which country I was living in, since I certainly didn't recognise it. The article proclaimed that Spanish banks were amazing, superb institutions of fidelity, honesty and helpfulness with zero corruption, as opposed to British banks, which were all corrupt, staffed by machines and assisted by hardened crooks as counter staff, although I exaggerate slightly here. The writer seemed to be totally overwhelmed that the bank staff in her branch were always the same people, knew her by name, indeed well enough to be greeted with a kiss, cuddle and coffee whenever she visits the bank, as well as being on close dinner party terms with the bank manager. I began to wonder whether it was a bar or a bank that the writer was talking about. Alarm bells rang and a vision of the corrupt bank manager working in the small town in Gran Canaria sprang to mind.

I use two banks regularly in Spain, and thankfully, I have no such relationship with my bank manager, nor am I ever greeted with a good morning kiss, cuddle and coffee. I do not know if the bank manager is a man or a woman, their name, or whether the branch has a manager at all; it really doesn't matter to me. The staff are continually changing, and although they are polite, it is rare that any work in the same branch for more than a few months.

No, it is not kisses, cuddles, coffee or dinner parties that I require from my bank, but a helpful, reliable service that meets my day-to-day needs. I like to use technology, so expect to be given reliable, online banking, together with an app for my iPhone to allow me to check and make transactions whenever I wish. I expect cash machines to work whenever I want one, and that there will be someone to assist me in person when I need help. I am more than happy to use telephone banking, and particularly if they can assist me in English. Yes, whilst I can deal with my bank quite happily in Spanish, I prefer to use my own language in health, legal and financial matters.

As for the British bank dimension, I certainly did not recognise that description either, since I have always found my British bank branch to be helpful, despite recently posting two cheques to the UK that were lost in the system. I had assumed that it was the fault of the Spanish postal service, but one cheque did eventually turn up at a credit card centre in London, which was a little surprising, since I had posted it to Newcastle. My only complaint is with the bank's telephone banking service, since I can rarely speak to anyone in their call centre who speaks anything but Punjabi, but that may be my hearing. However, in the bank's defence, my letter of complaint relating to the missing cheque met with a prompt and considered response, together with a nice credit, which paid for dinner out to compensate me for my trouble.

So, wherever we live in the World, I suspect that we will find both good and bad banks, with good and bad staff, good and bad systems, and those whose managers give kisses, cuddles and coffee and throw dinner parties, and those who do not. As with many expats, I am enthusiastic about my life in Spain and the Canary Islands. However, it is important to retain a balanced approach to our new lives, and not see everything in the expat garden through rose tinted wine glasses. It is also important to accept that because we have moved countries, life is suddenly not going to be wonderful in every way. Certainly, that is not my experience, and life continues to be one of endless surprises and challenges. Much depends upon our attitude to life, wherever we may live, and I wouldn't have it any other way.

The Birthday Expat

This is the time of year when I begin to dread yet another birthday. It's not that I don't appreciate being around for another year, because I do, but it is a time for reflection, as well as celebration. For me, these are times to reflect on those family members and friends who have passed on during the year, as well as remembering previous times spent together. My mind goes back to happy, as well as less happy, times spent with my parents, brothers, aunts and uncles and friends that make up so many memories, which help to form the fabric of our lives.

All of us see the pattern of life repeating through our friends and families, with engagements, weddings, new babies, some christenings (and not necessarily in that order), parties and all the patterns of celebration within family life that seem to be ingrained into our very psyche. I guess the passage of time is even more acute for expats when, because of distance, time and the high costs of travel, many of us do not see our families and friends as much as we would like. Many of our expat friends tell us that they often feel "excluded" from family events, not through deliberate intention, but just because people have their own busy lives, and time and events move rapidly on. I know of many expats who, when faced with the excitement and wonder of a newly-born grandchild, forgo their life in the sun and return to the UK; that family tie is often far too strong to resist.

As expats, we have chosen not to be part of the normal routines of family life. If we are fortunate, our families have moved with us, but if not, we are grateful for the special times that we can spend together, as well as being thankful for the occasional phone call, email, as well as contact through Facebook, Skype, WhatsApp and other social media.

It is also strange how time changes the way that people see us. Some years ago, I seemed to be receiving endless spam emails about sex toys and non-prescription drugs. A few years later, I started receiving emails about Viagra, which worried me in case they knew something that I didn't. Nowadays, I am receiving endless emails about funeral plans. I guess it is all part of life's rich tapestry...

Last week I was travelling by bus to Las Palmas, when I spotted an elderly woman who was struggling with her shopping. There were no seats available, and so I did what I always do in such circumstances; I stood up and offered the woman my seat. My parents taught me from an early age to always give up my seat to the elderly, infirm and pregnant women. It is a rule that I have always been guided by; however, on this occasion, it backfired spectacularly. The woman shook her head, thanked me and replied that I probably needed the seat more than she did. I sat down, thoroughly chastened, and determined that the time had probably come when I should sit tight, regardless of the aged and pregnant.

I find that the best way for me to cope with birthdays nowadays is by going away from home, which is a pattern that we have followed since becoming expats. I guess it is linked to not being able to be with family and friends from the past and the sometimes painful flood of memories at this time of the year. I have been blessed with a loving partner for many years, and it is a time when we enjoy sharing birthdays together, exploring and creating our own memories for the future. I'm just off to Lanzarote, which is this year's party island.

The Unfriendly Expat

During this UK pre-election period, most of us will come to realise that statistics can be adjusted to mean almost anything to anyone. It was therefore with some cynicism that I read a recent article where the authors claimed that "Nearly one third of British expats have no local friends and refuse to stray beyond the safety of their British friendship groups". The study went on to claim that only one in four expats would describe their social group as mainly British, with one in 10 admitting that their friends were exclusively British. Only 10 per cent of expats claimed to mix mainly with local people, and more than one third couldn't be bothered to learn the language, with a quarter admitting that they were not at all interested in the culture that they found themselves living in. The implied message from the article was, of course, that British expats living overseas are a miserable lot, whilst expats from other countries are so much friendlier and easier to talk to. It all made for rather shocking reading, but then I remembered to add a rather hearty pinch of salt that I usually reserve for some of the more outrageous British tabloids.

Integrating into a new community, trying to learn the language, however many mistakes, as well as appreciating the culture, is all part of the adventure and process of settling into a new home, a new community and a new country. Even though technology now means that it is easy to maintain contact with friends and family in the UK, it is local friends and neighbours who will be there to advise and to help in a crisis.

Admittedly, the attitude of the host country and its people also has an impact upon the happiness of the newly arrived expat and will help to determine how quickly expats settle. One survey claims that the vast majority of expats immediately feel at home in New Zealand, with similar responses from expats living in Canada. Again, it is the warmth of the welcome, and a shared language and culture that are the main factors for this result, but the same thing can happen in Spain, France, Italy and Portugal too.

So what relevance does all this data have upon the expat contemplating moving to or already living in Spain or another European country? It is true that expat life can sometimes revolve around mixing with and socialising with expats from the same country of origin. Much the same criticism can be said about the Germans, Swedish, Irish and Norwegians who often feel more comfortable and sheltered by their own communities, who are anxious to build their own churches, schools and hospitals, using only their own shops, restaurants and bars. Many British, Irish, German or Norwegian urbanisations that I visited as a reporter in Spain were clearly defended against perceived 'outsiders', including those from the host country.

As a newspaper reporter in Spain's Costa Blanca, I once had the misfortune to report upon the misery of one Spanish couple who were being ostracised by their mainly British neighbours, for being the only Spanish couple living in 'their urbanisation'. When I attempted to discover the reasons for the hostility, a range of complaints were thrown at me, including the couple having meals, drinking and partying late at night, playing loud Spanish music, their untidy garden, as well as parking in the wrong places. On the face of it, most were trivial complaints from a colony of Brits who preferred to be in bed by 10.30pm, and unwilling to adjust to the culture, timing and habits of residents from the host country. Sadly, I later discovered that the Spanish family could stand the unpleasantness no longer and moved away from the area. The expats had missed good opportunities to learn from their Spanish neighbours. If they had bothered to learn a little Spanish, much could have been resolved through friendly discussion, as a well as adopting more of a 'live and let live' attitude to their neighbours. It seemed that most of these expats were not happy people, and most would have been much happier living in Bognor Regis than in an expat urbanisation in the Costa Blanca.

On a more positive note, my own experiences of British expats is that most are more than happy to mix with their European neighbours, given the opportunity. Often, failure to mix is due to lack of motivation to learn the language, together with traditional British reserve and, unlike the article written around some rather suspect statistics, it has very little to do with a lack of willingness to make friends.

Healthy, Wealthy and Wise?

The Atlantic Travelling Butter Dish

It all began with a newspaper article in the online edition of my favourite newspaper, when I came across a report about the evils of eating margarine. Yes, you have read this correctly, because I seem to have read endless articles about the evils of butter and the benefits of margarine over the years. The article pointed out that margarine was originally developed as a product to quickly fatten turkeys in the USA. When the turkeys became ill and died, the manufacturers were left with so much margarine in their stores that they scratched their corporate heads in despair, asking themselves what they should do with their newly created margarine mountain. The answer was of course perfectly obvious, to feed it to humans instead.

I nearly dropped my piece of toast, which was liberally spread with expensive cholesterol reducing margarine and lovingly coated with Marmite. I read disturbing accounts about the margarine industry's efforts not only to turn the butter loving public away from this 'natural' food into eating a plastic substitute that was not fit for turkeys, believing that it was good for them. We have all been assured in the past that if we eat margarine instead of butter we would be less likely to have a heart attack or stroke, and recent promotions even claim to reduce cholesterol. What's not to like?

So, what has this to do with the butter dish and the Canary Islands, I hear you asking. Well, for many years I have been searching for a butter dish made by a manufacturer that ceased production many years ago, in order to complete a set of much loved tableware. In view of this article and many others, we decided to switch back to butter, in moderation, of course. Imagine my delight when I found a brand new butter dish from this manufacturer on an auction website. It was exactly what I wanted, and so I purchased it right away.

I was assured that the item would be despatched immediately and that I would receive it within a week. I was a little sceptical of this promise, having had many problems with parcel deliveries to the island in the past, and dreaded what the customs and delivery people would add as a "tax and service charge", but I remained optimistic. During the next six weeks, according to tracking, my butter dish crossed the Atlantic three times, and was finally returned to the suppliers in the UK as 'undeliverable'. Despite checking addresses, quoting National Identity numbers and all the rest of the bureaucracy that accompanies life on the island, the lady who dealt with my problem on behalf of the suppliers was charming, but finally admitted that a delivery to the Canary Islands "Had her beat", before adding, "Would you like a refund?"

Clearly, the Canary Islands do not welcome butter dishes. Having been down this route many times before with other items, and having learned never to give up. I arranged for the butter dish to be sent to a friend in the UK. From there, I will either collect it during my next visit to the UK, or ask one of our friends to bring it with them when they next visit the Canary Islands. I can then once again enjoy seeing butter in an attractive butter dish, instead of a plastic box. Yes, I guess we all have our little obsessions in life.

Meanwhile, if you would like more information about the evils of margarine, I suggest a little first hand research on Google along the lines of "butter versus margarine". Recent research studies may surprise and shock you.

Drinking Foggy Water

I have always been a little cynical about the value of bottled water. It always irritates me when a waiter tries to palm me off with an expensive bottle of 'French Mountain Spring' water, when there are perfectly good bottled waters available in the Canary Islands. Not only is it a travesty for the carbon footprint linked to any product, but why is French bottled water better than anyone else's?

Of course the answer is commercialisation and profit. Over the years we have been led to believe that bottled water is somehow better for us than the water running freely from our taps, although I accept that use of a water purifier and filter is always a good idea to avoid stomach upsets. Yes, the addition of a fancy label and a posh French-sounding name adds up to quite an expensive bottle of water.

A few years ago I had the good fortune to spend an entertaining evening with an engineer who worked for a water company in London. His description of the chemical composition of tap water, including the side effects caused by some of the chemicals that cannot be removed, which can lead to the development of impressive breasts in men, led me to look at bottled water in a new light. It was then that I discovered the joys of mountain mist.

Mountain mist is collected from the highest peaks of the Canary Islands, which is now being bottled and sold as drinking water. It is collected on the island of Gran Canaria from fog at altitudes of 16,000 metres above sea level and sold under the brand name of

Alisios, which is the name given to chilly, damp tropical winds that give the Canary Islands their typical climate at high altitudes. As much as 20,000 litres of clean water is collected from the mist in 30 prism shaped containers each month. This cool, steamy mist is sold as 'Canarian Mist Water', a process that is also kind to the environment since it leaves no waste and there are no emissions from the process.

It seems that the collection of mountain mist for use in this way is not new since there are accounts of similar water collection processes in historical accounts that date back a mere 2000 years. Pliny the Elder gives an account of the Garoe tree being 'milked' in a similar manner, which filled man-made ponds – a kind of early reservoir. The water collected provided drinking water in an area with no rivers. More recently, in 1948, a man from the island of El Hierro avoided a devastating drought by collecting water 'milked' from trees in zinc containers, which was then sold to villagers.

So next time you are offered an expensive bottle of 'French Mountain Spring' water in a pricey restaurant, maybe ask for a bottle of Canarian Mountain Mist water instead? That should stop the waiter in his tracks.

Healthcare for Expats in Spain and the Canary Islands

Expats can be a strange lot. A great deal of time is often spent in selecting the right place to live, a new home, kitchen appliances and even thinking about a new job. However, I rarely find that expats give much consideration to that most important of subjects - healthcare. Indeed, along with "How do I get Brit TV?" one of the most popular questions that I am asked, often when it is too late, is "Can I get free healthcare in Spain?" Of course, the answer is a confusing yes, and … no.

When I worked as a reporter in the Costa Blanca, I remember interviewing a couple who had retired early and moved to Spain long before the statutory retirement age when the man would have been entitled to free healthcare within the Spanish health system for both he and his wife. They were unhappy that their Spanish doctor had refused them treatment and wanted the newspaper to publish a story condemning the "injustice", as they saw it, when they were refused treatment. The couple were rather proud of the fact that they would travel back to the UK every six months to collect their "free E111 health certificate", which at that time would allow them to claim free emergency medical treatment in Spain. The couple seemed to be hypochondriacs, so when they were in the UK, they, mother in law and assorted family members would enjoy free UK NHS care, before continuing their treatment free within the Spanish system when they returned home.

Eventually, this state of affairs came to a sticky end, when their Spanish doctor eventually realised what was going on and refused to treat them under the free E111 scheme, which was only ever intended to be reciprocal emergency cover for holidaymakers. The couple were not at all happy and after much complaining, reluctantly opted to take out rather expensive private health cover until he reached the statutory retirement age. I remember listening sympathetically to the story, but with no intention of publishing it. At a time of scarce health resources, I thought it was admirable of the doctor to spot abuse of the system, and to do something about it.

Clearly, this was pure abuse of an already overstretched system, and governments of both countries were right to put an end to it. In more recent years, the financial crisis faced by all countries in Europe have forced governments to reassess exactly who qualifies for free or subsidised treatment and who does not. Of course, many have fallen foul of the new rules, leaving some without any health cover at all, and often because they do not understand the newly enforced requirements.

In the case of Spain, the message is clear. If you are an expat over the statutory retirement age, you will be entitled to free healthcare, but always check your entitlement with the Department of Health in the UK before you move to Spain. If you are under the statutory retirement age and have a contract of employment, your employers will usually provide free healthcare under the Spanish system, but do check that this is the case.

If neither is applicable, you have two options. The first is to purchase private health insurance. This can be expensive, dependent upon any pre-existing conditions and age. Although I have private health insurance, I am not a great fan of private healthcare, and would not wish to rely upon it for everything. It is reassuring to have it for emergency referrals and second opinions, but I am an admirer of both the UK and Spanish Health Services, which would always be my preferred choice in most circumstances.

If you are not entitled to free Spanish NHS cover, you can now purchase it within most of the autonomous regions of Spain. It is very good value with cover in the Canary Islands, for instance, now available for 60 euros per month. This does, however, exclude subsidised prescriptions, which have to be paid for in full, and the European health card (EHIC) if you wish to travel to other countries. However, as most expats quickly recognise, most generic drugs are exceptionally good value in Spain, and far cheaper than their equivalents in the UK.

In conclusion, if you are not retired, or in full time employment with a contract that includes health insurance, I recommend buying into the Spanish NHS scheme (Convenio Especial), as well as supplementing it with private insurance cover, if you can afford it. It is one of those things that may be irritating, boring and time consuming to arrange, but you will be very grateful for it should the time come to use it.

Fight Alzheimer's - Learn a Language!

I often hear expats complaining about the difficulties of learning Spanish, despite being well aware that their experiences as an expat would be greatly enhanced by making the effort to communicate in the language of their new country. Sadly, many fail in the process, despite their best efforts and sometimes through no fault of their own.

Ideally, expats should have a working knowledge of the language before they even set foot in their newly adopted country. How often did we hear during the UK election campaign, for instance, politicians and the public complaining about immigrants arriving in the UK without a working knowledge of the language? This lack of ability to communicate creates barriers, suspicion and resentment, and is one of the many reasons why immigration can become such a divisive issue in any community. Life is not predictable, and for most expats, learning a language is a long and continuing process upon arrival. However, it can be fun and it is a willingness to try that is important.

I have often heard, and read reports indicating that learning a language after the age of fifty is very difficult, although many good teachers will dispute this. Certainly, the quality of teaching, materials used, enthusiasm and a willingness to learn are all part of the ingredients of any learning, be it with others in a group, as an individual, in small group lessons, or simply following a recorded language course.

I vividly remember that as a newly arrived expat in Spain, I signed up for a language course funded and promoted by the municipality. I attended the first evening with great enthusiasm until I met the other 39 newly arrived expats in my class. The pointlessness and frustration of trying to learn for an hour in a class of 40 middle aged people of varying ability was sad to experience, and is only successful in putting people off learning a new language. Indeed, a few weeks later when I checked what was going on, the class size had reduced to just five people. Maybe this was the overall intention, but it is a very sad and destructive way to promote learning of a language.

Despite the difficulties and frustrations when learning a new language, there is also plenty of good news. A recent report claims that using Spanish in everyday situations, as well as regularly attending classes, can help to prevent or delay the onset of Alzheimer's disease. The research claims that the first signs of dementia can be delayed by at least five years by learning a language.

Expats living in Spain are certainly at an advantage, and are most likely to benefit since those who regularly use the language are even more likely to fight off Alzheimer's than those who have merely studied a language in isolation in their home country and then fail to use it in day-to-day situations.

Doctors have claimed for many years that thinking activities, such as Sudoku and crosswords help to ward off confusion and memory loss in old age. In addition, specialists claim that those who speak two or more languages have an even stronger chance of retaining their mental faculties. Well, I can take a hint; I'm just off for my Chinese lesson.

Go On, Unzip a Banana!

I was chatting to a banana grower friend the other day. He was very concerned, because the banana growers of the Canary Islands have recently threatened industrial action. They feel undervalued and underpaid, and they are concerned that with cheaper imports entering the European Union from other countries, their livelihoods are being threatened. Despite the islands' tourism industry, the growing of fruit and vegetables, and particularly the banana, remain an essential part of the Canary Islands' economy, which should not be underestimated.

Many visitors comment about the fields of polythene sheeting that adorn the sides of many roads in the Canary Islands. As well as protecting soft fruit and vegetables, many such structures shelter bananas from the ravages of the strong Atlantic winds. Our garden is surrounded by several very large and impressive banana plants that brush noisily against the wall in strong winds, which reminds me of the importance of the banana to these islands.

I am a great fan of the humble banana, particularly if it is the traditional Canarian variety, as opposed to those huge, tasteless, perfectly shaped objects usually found in most UK supermarkets. The Canarian banana is well worth searching out, and some of the better UK supermarkets now stock them. Although smaller in size, they are full of flavour and are much sweeter and creamier than the imported bananas from the Caribbean, which are often picked too early, artificially ripened and sprayed with gas to control the ripening process.

I am always surprised that bananas are not more popular; after all, they are nature's energy bar, which is far better for you than one of those expensive sports drinks. Although maybe not as 'cool' as a heavily advertised 'sports drink', one medium sized banana contains around ten per cent of the daily potassium intake that most adults need.

These fresh, creamy fruits from the Canary Islands are cheap and readily available throughout the year. They are rich in calories, with 100 grams of fruit containing around 90 calories, as well as being rich in anti-oxidants, minerals and vitamins. Its flesh is made up of simple sugars, such as sucrose and fructose that instantly replenish the body, and is why they are so popular with athletes. The amount of soluble dietary fibre also means that it is good for the bowels, which means that you can avoid constipation by eating regular supplies of bananas. Now that really must be good news.

This humble fruit also contains a generous helping of Vitamin B6, which helps to treat inflammation of the nerves and anaemia, as well as helping to prevent coronary artery disease and stroke. A portion of fruit also contains a dose of Vitamin C, which helps to ward off some of those nasty diseases, magnesium for strengthening bones, and copper for helping in the production of red blood cells. What's not to like?

In short, this wonderful fruit helps to combat depression, cures hangovers, helps to protect against kidney cancer, diabetes, osteoporosis and blindness. Bananas are the only raw fruit that can be eaten to relieve stomach ulcers, because they coat the lining of the stomach against corrosive acids. By the way, you can also rub a banana over a mosquito bite to sooth the pain and disinfect the wound and, if you really must, you can use one to clean your shoes. I wish the plants growing over my garden wall would hurry up and give me some fruit.

Open Wide!

I received an invitation to visit the dentist today. Nothing unusual in that maybe, since I seem to have had a rapid succession of appointments with the dentist since that unfortunate incident with a peanut and excessive turbulence on an internal flight in the Canary Islands last summer. No, this dental appointment is different; it is an invitation to attend a celebration of ten years of the dental practice opening, which fortunately coincided with our arrival in Gran Canaria.

At that time I remember tentatively calling into a newly opened surgery in our nearest town to get some details of the dental care that was available. The surgery appeared to be brimming with the latest technology and what seemed to be high tech equipment that was far removed from the small, quaint practice that I usually attended in the UK. I remember being impressed not only with the equipment, but a more sensible regime for appointments, routine cleaning, as well as a clear pricing structure. Indeed, the fees seemed to be about half of those that I paid in the UK.

Some years ago, I remember many friends and relatives in the UK commenting that they now had a Spanish dentist, working both in private practice, as well as filling the many gaps in the NHS dental service. Even though I was pleased for UK patients, I began to wonder if this would lead to a shortage of dentists in Spain and the Canary Islands, which did seem to be a possibility.

Due to changes in the fee structure for dentists in the UK, many dentists were leaving the National Health Service, and provided care for private patients only. This shortage of dentists tempted many newly qualified, as well as established, Spanish dentists to leave Spain in order to fill the acute gaps within the UK's dental service. This began to cause a problem for Spain's own dental service, resulting in shortages of qualified dentists. This situation coincided with an excess of dentists being trained in South America, and particularly in Argentina, which had rapidly expanded its dental training programme, as well as developing new dental techniques such as dental implants, resulting in far too many dentists for the country to absorb. This was fortunate, because many newly trained dentists left South America and headed to Spain and the Canary Islands to work in established surgeries, as well as opening their own.

My own dentist is also from Argentina and until recently was one of the few dental surgeons in Spain who was sufficiently qualified to deal with dental implants. When I first knew him, he used to work for two days each week in Madrid and three days in Gran Canaria until his own practice became sufficiently well established. Since that time, the dental surgery has grown and rapidly expanded, resulting in much larger premises, as well as a new sister surgery opening in Las Palmas. The care that we have received has been second to none, and I am grateful that I stumbled across a good dentist during those first heady days of our new life in Gran Canaria. Now that is something to celebrate and it will be so good to visit my dentist for celebratory drinks and nibbles instead of a new crown or a filling!

Money Doesn't Buy Happiness, but it Helps

I have just finished speaking to a friend in the UK. It is mid-August, and he told me that he and his family have had to spend the whole day indoors. Anyone with young children will know how tiresome this can be when there isn't even a small break in the rain to allow for a brief walk or a kick around in the nearest park. Apparently, the month that most Brits look forward to all year had been pretty grim, and the forecast did not look as if it would improve anytime soon. I put the phone down, feeling concerned for our friend, who works exceptionally long hours, is highly stressed and continually juggles his life to please everyone. I wandered outdoors and poured another glass of wine.

It was about 9 o'clock and we had just settled down to our meal outside. It was a lovely warm evening with a clear sky. I could hear neighbours chatting and laughing, as well as smelling yet another meal of barbecued fish, an odour that I really detest. However, there was a gentle breeze and the cooking would not last for long. It was an evening that was typical for us, as well as for many neighbours and friends living in the Canary Islands and Spain.

The differences between our life in the sun and that of our friend in the UK could not have been starker, and our conversation reminded me of a recent report by the OECD, in which Spain fell only just behind Denmark in a ranking of work-life balance, in a study of the world's advanced economies. Spanish people devote a larger portion of their day to personal care and leisure than any other country in the world, including Denmark, with more than 16 hours each day devoted to eating, hobbies and meeting friends. This statistic did not surprise me, since Spain's ability to maintain a healthy work-life balance has been known for many years.

The report stresses the importance of achieving a good work-life balance and that the ability to combine family commitments, work, and wellbeing is important for everyone. Failure to achieve this and working long hours may impair personal health and increase stress, as well as jeopardising safety.

Although Spain ranked above average in its work-life balance, as well as in housing, community and health, the country lagged at the bottom of the charts, along with Greece, for jobs, with very high levels of unemployment, and particularly for 18- to 25-year-olds nationally, and with even more appalling levels of unemployment in the Canary Islands. This score dragged down the overall ranking for Spain, with Spaniards less happy with their lives than those in other countries, ranking just 6.5 on a scale of 1 to 10, when compared with an average of 6.6.

Despite Denmark leading the way in overall life satisfaction, followed by Iceland, Switzerland, Norway and Israel, not all benefit from a good, healthy climate, or peace and security, which Spain enjoys.

Despite the riches of a glorious climate, sensible working hours, a good health and education service, the ability to work and earn a decent living is an essential ingredient in the path to true happiness.

Boys' and Girls' Toys

The Canary Islander

Boys' Toys

I like toys as much as the next man. Be it train sets, steam cars, remote control helicopters, iPhones or Nintendo. Other, sometimes questionable, gadgets have also come onto the market in recent years, including devices for treasure hunting on the beach and public areas. I received an email from an American gentleman last week who said that he had been so inspired by 'Letters from the Atlantic' that he wanted to move to the Canary Islands. He had but one question to ask before he made his move. He asked whether or not he would be allowed to use his metal detector on the beaches of the islands.

These gadgets are, of course, frowned upon by many who regard them as merely looting the coins and jewellery of unfortunate souls who have lost them during a day out on the beach. Others will say that these treasure seekers have the potential to unearth historical artefacts from the past, although whether this is for the public good, or for personal gain, is an on going debate. I replied that I thought that he should investigate whether or not he is able to gain residency to the country before he worries too much about treasure hunting. Somehow, I think his priorities were a little distorted.

As for current gadgets, I have been a little surprised at the sudden interest in personal drones. For the uninitiated, drones are a kind of upgraded remote control helicopter that hovers wherever the operator directs it, with many sporting a camera that happily takes photos or even videos of the world below. It is supposed to be a hi-tech toy, but it does take remote surveillance to an entirely new level.

My first encounter with a real life drone was one hovering over the outdoor swimming pool in our village. At first I was fascinated to watch this amazing piece of technology hovering just a few metres from where locals and myself were swimming and sunbathing. However, the more I thought about it the more I realised that the unintended consequences of this tiny flying machine could be very serious, particularly if carrying a camera on board. Hovering over public swimming pools and beaches taking photographs and videos could be seen as a pornographers' paradise, and when involving children is potentially much more serious.

Then there is home security. Is your terrace or garden shielded from prying eyes? Clearly a hovering drone could easily become a public nuisance with its irritating buzzing and intrusive nature. As I said earlier, I adore new technology of all kinds, but I am also a great shot with a catapult, a widely unrecognised skill of mine that I picked up during many boring lunch hours when I was at school. Let me be quite clear, should I spot a drone hovering over my garden it will suddenly find itself shot down into oblivion. After all, wherever in the world we may live, an expat Englishman's home is his castle.

Techie Toys for Expats: Stay Smart with DNS

As a newly arrived or intending expat, you will be given many pieces of advice; some will be useful, whilst it is best to ignore others. The best piece of advice is, of course, to learn the language, because by doing so you will add a new depth and valuable dimension to your new life in the sun. The second piece of advice that I often hear is to only watch TV and listen to radio in the language of your adopted country. In other words, forget 'Eastenders' and 'Strictly Come Dancing', in favour of some of the endless quiz and reality shows on Spanish television; I think not. I have come to the opinion that to remain in touch with the language and culture of birth is important, which helps to ease some of the lonelier and unsettling aspects of expat life, even if the sun is shining. So, in order to continue to enjoy watching 'Coronation Street' and 'Dr Who', and films in your home language, it is important to be able to watch television from your home country.

One of the most frequent questions that I am asked by both would be and newly arrived expats is "Will I still be able to watch British television?" Although not strictly legal, the answer is "Yes, of course you will, and things are getting better all the time." However, you do need to be a little tech savvy to ensure that you are getting the best connection, and that doesn't necessarily mean spending a great deal of money on monthly TV contracts.

When we first moved to Spain, the choice was either

installing a large and expensive satellite dish, or having a baking tray kind of contraption strapped to the highest point of the building. Both systems worked, but were not always reliable, since providers and connections changed and, indeed, satellites moved to other positions, which required adjustments, upgrades and yet more expense. Over the last few years, things have moved on, and it is now perfectly possible to receive a good television signal from your Internet connection; indeed, it is now the preferred choice for many reasons.

Watching television through your Internet connection doesn't mean sitting in front of your laptop all evening. We now have the option of purchasing Internet ready TVs, although my own personal preference is using a computer (in my case a Mac Mini) linked specifically to our main television for only Internet television and film viewing.

Of course, television programmes from the UK and other countries are blocked, to prevent them from being watched in other countries. However, there are many ways around this. Until recently, my preferred option has been the use of a Virtual Private Network (VPN), which basically tricks the television provider into thinking that you are in your home country. The signal is diverted to your home country and then forwarded back to the sender. Clearly, the downside of this process is that VPN reduces your signal by around 30 per cent, reducing picture quality or producing that maddening buffering, and spinning 'circle of death' that we all hate so much. In many parts of the Canary Islands where I live, and rural Spain, France, Italy and Portugal, Internet signals are very slow offering maybe only 3 to 10mbps. I am fortunate, since I now have a connection called VDSL (Very High Bit Rate DSL), which offers a speed of around 30mbps. Even so, I managed to get a decent signal on a speed of only 10mbps. It is important to shop around and obtain the highest speed possible. Try to request VDSL if a fibre optic connection is unavailable in your area; it is a little more expensive, but well worth it. Secondly, if you can afford it, dump the modem and router provided by your telecoms provider, since most are of the most basic quality and purchase the best, high-speed version modem/router that you can afford. It will be worth it in the long run, since speed is the key to success.

My much-preferred option now is Smart DNS, which is simply a case of changing the DNS numbers on your computer or router. It sounds complicated, but isn't and full details of how to do this are given by the company providing the service. Smart DNS has the advantage of maintaining the full strength of your signal, which in areas with low Internet signal strength is highly important, but has the disadvantage of not being secure in the same way as VPN. My best advice is to get both, and then you can use Smart DNS to receive television programmes, access films etc., whilst using VPN for security and to hide your presence if, for instance, you are using your laptop in an Internet cafe to access your bank account.

For space reasons, I cannot go into more details in this article, but you can find more information, as well as details about the companies and products that I use, on the Expat Survival section of my website.

Twitter Town

I have to admit it, but I am not a great lover of Twitter. To be honest, I don't really understand it. I can see the point of Facebook, which as an expat has helped me to keep in contact with friends and family that I have not seen for some time. It is great fun reading lively posts, and viewing amusing photos and videos, although I do find the "I'm all hung over this morning" posts and the "Look what I'm eating now" photos a tad irritating. After all, do we really wish to witness the cause of many a stomach upset? Anyway, my favourite posts are of cats and dogs getting up to all sorts of strange antics. I like dolphins too.

Although I use Twitter, in the sense that it is automatically linked to my weekly posts, it is not a format that I understand or like. My main gripe is why on earth would someone willingly restrict themselves to such a pathetic number of characters when the English language is so deliciously rich and colourful? It is impossible to say what you really mean in such a pathetically small number of words. I am always surprised that Stephen Fry, who has grown into something of a 'national treasure', has anything to do with it. Yes, I know that many will disagree, but I am just saying...

It was therefore with some surprise that friends in Granada recently alerted me to a news item about the activities in a nearby small Spanish town, Jun, which now uses Twitter as a way of administering the city's public services. Indeed, should you enter this small town, you will be greeted by an obelisk in the centre of a roundabout, decorated with the famous Twitter bird logo. The chief Twitterite of the town, Mayor Jose Antonio Rodriguez Salas, has been experimenting with this form of social media for a number of years and now claims that Twitter has allowed the city authorities to eliminate bureaucracy. Full marks to the Mayor, since he claims that all the paperwork is now done on Twitter, and that all 3,500 residents of Jun should have a Twitter account to join in the fun. So far, he has around 600 converts registered with the Town Hall, which allows them to make doctor's appointments, book rooms at the town hall, report crimes, non-functioning street lamps, as well as tweeting about the quality of school lunches.

For those who cannot quite grasp the system, Twitter courses are available, allowing residents to take part in town hall meetings, using tweets of course. Apparently, the town's road sweeper is now something of a celebrity too, because he receives many congratulatory tweets appreciating his work. I do wonder how he feels about jobs that are not so well done, but then again, I am all for instant feedback.

The police service is something that concerns me since the Mayor proudly proclaims that he has managed to reduce the police force from four to one police officer; I guess that went down a treat with the union. Presumably, the one remaining officer spends all day replying to tweets... Anyway, do it yourself policing is clearly the way forward in Jun, and relatively easy now that Jun has free Wi-Fi Internet access throughout the town. If you do catch a thief, just send a tweet to the town's one remaining police officer; he will be far too busy to appear in person, but you will get a nice, but brief, reply. Twitter is free, immediate and efficient, which ticked all of the Mayor's boxes for a quality public service.

Twitter itself were also keen to get in on the action when they heard about the way that their service was being used, leading to a visit from Twitter's chief data scientist, who was fascinated by the way that Jun was using social media for the public good. He acknowledged that, as with all good things, not everyone in Jun is willing to take part, which did come as a bit of a blow. Twitter meanwhile, are looking at how Jun's example could be extended to New York, San Francisco, Chicago and, indeed, the World.

Whilst I applaud the Mayor's enthusiasm and the development of technology for the social good, I do have some minor concerns about the lack of real social interaction, confidentiality in the case of medical appointments, the reduction of policing to just one man with a phone, but can see the point of immediate reporting of issues, such as the quality of school lunches, as well as congratulating the street cleaner. As for me, all this talk of Twitter has driven me back to my typewriter. Yes, the World is going quietly mad…

The Viewfinder Blues

As a primary school teacher, I had the privilege of reading and listening to a vast number of fairy and folk tales with children for many years. It always surprised me how moral and relevant many of these stories are to adult life, and I often find myself linking modern day events to one of those very early stories.

One such story is the one about 'The Emperor's New Clothes'. The story is about a very vain, and often cruel, Emperor who insists upon having the very latest, best and most expensive in high fashion. The Emperor is surrounded by sycophants, courtiers and citizens, who agree with everything that the foolish man says for fear of harsh reprisals, but no one ever actually tells him the truth. On one occasion, the Emperor ordered the 'finest of all bespoke garments' from a visiting 'master tailor'. The vain man was so pleased with result that he strutted out onto the palace balcony in his new garments for all to see. The crowd cheered and clapped their approval, but a small boy in the crowd finally revealed the ghastly truth that the Emperor was wearing no clothes at all. The 'finest of all bespoke garments' was actually a con, and the Emperor was, in fact, completely naked. It had taken one innocent child to actually reveal the truth.

I have always been interested in photography and I have collected a number of cameras over the years. The problem is that all these cameras are large and I really need one that I can slip into my pocket for those unexpected occasions and 'once in a lifetime' shots. For some years, everyone has told me to buy one of the very small, digital jobs that will slip into the tiniest of places, yet produce superb photos. These cameras may be excellent in many ways, but they all have one big deficiency, none have a viewfinder, and I cannot see a thing. Sadly, camera manufacturers stopped making small cameras with viewfinders some years ago, because moving to the large rear camera screen is "progress" and no one wants a viewfinder in their cameras nowadays. I have tried many modern digital cameras over the last few years, and have come to the same conclusion, that without a viewfinder, and having to rely on a small screen in sunlight to compose a picture is a joke, yet I have never really liked to admit it.

Many have suggested that I rely on my smartphone as a camera. Again, regardless of brand, I am faced with exactly the same issue; I simply cannot see a thing on the screen in bright sunlight. Somehow, pointing in the vague direction of something that may be of interest, without being able to focus, zoom in closely and compose the shot has rather killed my interest in photography.

It is only in the last few weeks that I have finally discovered cameras made by several companies that now include a digital viewfinder in addition to the dreaded screen that I find so useless. Currently, this is not a widely advertised feature, as I am told that there would be "very little demand for a viewfinder nowadays". How wrong they are, as not only can I now see what I am looking at in the viewfinder; I can actually compose the shot, zoom in and out, as well as being able to adjust the settings in the same way that I could in the cameras of long ago. At last, some manufacturers have seen sense and are producing what some consumers actually need.

Back to the story of the Emperor's New Clothes. It is interesting that whenever I now tell people about my new camera and the way it has regenerated my interest in photography, as well as producing better quality results, I usually get a big smile, a sigh of relief and the comment, "I have the same problem. Where can I get one?"

I guess the moral of the story is that often we go along with the crowd for fear of making ourselves look foolish, whereas it is often far better to stand out from the crowd and tell it how it really is.

Viaduct Power

Ten years ago, an imaginative project began on the small Canary Island of El Hierro, which many thought would be impossible. It was an experiment that has the potential to be of enormous significance upon the global battle against climate change, and the abandonment of fossil fuels as a source of energy. This project has culminated in El Hierro now being totally self sufficient in energy by using the island's vast resources of wind and hydropower, involving a wind farm, hydroelectric plant, an efficient pumping system and two reservoirs.

One year ago, and before the big switchover, the island's 10,000 residents had to rely upon regular, and sometimes unreliable, shipments of oil from its larger neighbours. Now, on a typical windy day, more power is generated than required by its residents, and the excess power pumps water from one reservoir to another at a higher elevation of 700 metres. When the wind dies, the water is released to spin turbines to generate electricity. Planning and implementation has been a long and expensive process, costing around 82 million euros, but as the regional government and the island's inhabitants have been spending millions of euros each year on diesel, the long-term saving will be considerable. It is a project that has received attention from scientists and government specialists from many counties in a bid to resolve energy and pollution issues in their own countries.

Ten years on, I am still wondering why, on the neighbouring islands to El Hierro, we still have huge oil tankers feeding the power stations? Why have we not moved towards the El Hierro solution? As I live only a few kilometres from an electricity generating station in Gran Canaria, I am used to seeing tankers thundering down the small roads several times each day. The costs are enormous; roads are damaged, as well as the sheer inconvenience in shipping oil to the islands from the Spanish Peninsular to be fed into the power stations upon which we all rely.

Despite the success of solar energy, wind and wave power in many parts of the world, I rarely see solar panels on the roofs of businesses and government buildings, let alone residential homes on the island. We enjoy very high levels of sunshine throughout the year, and we have plenty of wind and wave energy surrounding the islands, but these natural resources are wasted. Instead, the oil companies prefer to scour the seas off these beautiful islands for deposits of oil and gas with scant regard to the damage that inevitably occurs to marine life. Fortunately, the price of oil has fallen to make this no longer economically viable, but only for the time being. We do have some wind turbines onshore, which I am rather fond of. After all, I would much rather live next to a wind farm than a nuclear power station or an oil refinery.

Remembering the huge anger generated about onshore wind farms in the UK, I read with interest a study by a team of Spanish and British researchers concerned with using spare space on skyscrapers, motorways and bridges to mount relatively unobtrusive wind turbines. Several test sites were considered, including the Juncal Viaduct in Gran Canaria. Using computer simulations, the researchers discovered that installing just two medium sized turbines between the bridge's existing pillars would produce power equivalent to 24 small wind turbines, which would be sufficient to meet the average power consumption of 450 to 500 homes on the island. The architect design of this 'revised' viaduct is not only impressive, but rather beautiful.

Sadly, there are no immediate plans to put these imaginative ideas into practice, but the research into the Juncal Viaduct has shown that, technically, it is possible. All we need now is political will, investment and a willingness to move away from oil, if the powerful oil companies and governments will allow it. The island of El Hierro has already proven that even the wildest dreams are possible, when having the will and determination to succeed.

Party Time

The Non-designer Christmas Tree

We are often told that "design is everything" and it is certainly true that if a product is appealing to the eye, functional and works as intended, sales may react accordingly. Black Friday, Cyber Monday and all the other pre-Christmas nonsense aside, I enjoy looking at Christmas trees and decorations. Stepping inside a shopping centre, large stores and small shops can be a feast to the eye with beautifully designed, co-ordinated Christmas trees adorned with bows, balls and tinsel.

On December 6 each year, our Christmas tree appears for the festive season. Those who see our tree will probably think it is anything but colour coordinated or carefully designed. It is a cacophony of colour, with decorations made from a wide variety of materials, and of all different shapes and sizes. Some of the decorations span well into the previous century since they have been handed down over several generations. Our tree represents a lifetime of our own personal memories, as well as from those who have gone before us. The oldest item is a sugar biscuit, which I was told used to adorn my great grandparents' Christmas tree.

We do not call our tree a Christmas tree, but a 'Memory Tree'. The beginning of our Christmas is careful decoration of the tree, recalling what the various items mean to us, where they came from and what has happened to the people who gave us the ornaments or small trinkets; it can be a lengthy process only interrupted by the odd mince pie and glass of our favourite malt whisky. Family, friends past and present, neighbours, gifts from pupils, colleagues, as well as items that my partner and I have collected over many years together find a place on the 'Memory Tree'. If we have not collected anything together during the year on our travels, we make a point of buying a small item before Christmas that means something special to both of us.

The usual baubles that I remember hanging on our family tree as a child with my mother, are now joined by glass angels, a distinctive blue and white Delft bear from Amsterdam, a china gondola from Venice, a wooden tram carriage from San Francisco, which contrast with a white swan beautifully made from a length of white ribbon by an elderly lady who visited my school weekly to help pupils with their reading. There are toy bears and knitted robins made by past pupils, a giraffe from South Africa, together with several beautiful toys, intended for a charity sale, made by my partner's mother. The last, and particularly special item to be added to the top of our 'Memory Tree' is a rather worse-for-wear fairy, given to me by my favourite aunt for my first Christmas. Some would refer to the collection of bits and pieces on our 'Memory Tree' as 'clutter', but they are the ones who do not know the many stories that each represents. 'Designer' it certainly is not, nor is there an ornate bow to be seen.

One of the most poignant memories this year will be hanging a beautiful decoration on the tree given to us by a close friend who died earlier this year. When he gave it to us, he knew that it would be his last Christmas. His final visit to our home was when he arrived just before Christmas clutching a small, beautifully wrapped box. We could see that buying it had given him great pain and effort in travelling to his favourite store. As usual with our friend, it was a gift well chosen. As he handed it to us, he said very little, but we knew that it was his last gift to us - a beautiful memory of him for the future.

With Black Friday and Cyber Monday now behind us, it is time for us to enjoy Christmas in our own special ways. We all have unique ways of celebrating the Christmas season. For some it will be for its religious significance, for others it will time for a good 'booze up', eating far too much food and partying with friends, and others will be enjoying a quiet time with their families. However, many people will be on their own, either through choice or because they have no one to share the holiday season with. I hope that they, in particular, will use their memories from happier times to comfort and sustain them through what can be a painful time of the year. However you choose to enjoy the Christmas season, may it be one that creates many happy memories for the future.

Pancakes, Vicars and Tarts

Thankfully, few Canarians have anything to do with pancakes, which are very much a British and American thing. However, despite not having a 'Pancake Day' in quite the same way as in the UK, Canarians still enjoy the day, as well as quite a few days before and after, known as 'Mardi Gras', which means 'Fat Tuesday', or 'Shrove Tuesday'. It is a time to really let your hair down before the gloomy period of self imposed penitence and repentance, known by Christians as Lent. Mardi Gras is a strange mixture of carnival, culture, tradition and religion, with the odd bit of debauchery thrown in for good measure. I guess this why so many people enjoy it, and its larger excesses are usually forgiven and forgotten.

The self-imposed frugality of Lent is, thankfully, demanded far less by the Church nowadays, although for many, it is still a period of self reflection, denial and rededication. As with New Year resolutions, many people decide to "give up something" for Lent. Often, this consists of taking a 'gentle approach' by denying oneself certain types of food, such as chocolate, or a biscuit with morning coffee, whilst others may choose to take 'the big bang approach' by giving up Facebook, shaving, alcohol or, as one of my friends is insisting upon this year, carbon emissions. The practicality of this last choice has yet to be explained to me. Personally, I much prefer taking the 'alternative approach' of having a really good party during 'Mardi Gras', and not worrying too much about the period of self-denial during the following forty days; there's plenty of time to worry about such things when we are dead.

During the week before the beginning of Lent, carnivals take place throughout the world, with some of the brightest, most unusual, biggest and best taking place in Spain and, in particular in the Canary Islands. All of the inhabited islands and most towns have their own versions of carnival, with those in Las Palmas de Gran Canaria, as well as in Santa Cruz de Tenerife, which are billed as "Second Only to Rio", offering some of the most spectacular experiences that residents, expats and visitors will never forget.

Annoyingly, unlike Christmas, Mardi Gras, Ash Wednesday and Lent can fall anytime between February 3rd and March 9th each year, since Easter is a moveable feast involving a calculation originally determined by the Catholic Church. As a result, Mardi Gras in many countries can hit a wet, cold period, or a deliciously warm one, which is usually the case in the Canary Islands. However, an early Mardi Gras does explain why many of the islands' young men, who tend to dress up as half naked angels, found the evenings so chilly this year.

The party is almost over, and costumes are being packed away as Carnival ends for another year. It grinds to a heady conclusion with a ritual funeral, called 'The Burial of the Sardine', in which a huge model of a sardine, accompanied by wailing, slutty widows, which some describe as a huge 'Vicars and Tarts Party', but with more dildos and greater blasphemy, is finally laid to rest. Does any of this make sense? Not really, but does it have to? In any case, it is great fun and if you haven't, you should try it sometime. It certainly blows away the winter blues!

Wine and Sex in the Canary Islands

It may seem an unlikely story, but the relatively recent popularity of wines from the Canary Islands came about as a result of 'Wine and Sex' parties organised by a local entrepreneur, who seemed to have an obsession, or fascination, with Tuppersex parties, which are based upon the highly successful concept of Tupperware parties. Instead of those delightful, sealable, plastic boxes, it was sex toys that were on offer. This operation seemed ideal for the introduction of a heady mix of sex toys and Canarian wines to titivate those with money and nothing better to do, which many experts say was the start of the boom in wines from the Canary Islands.

At first sight, the Canary Islands seem an unlikely source for some of the excellent wines produced today, since it is the most tropical of wine regions in Europe. Those who doubt the success of these wines should remember that back in the 15th century, sweet wines from the Canary Islands were hugely popular, both in the UK and Germany. Indeed, Shakespeare had a thing or two to say about this sweet wine, then called Malmsey, in his plays; for example, in 'Twelfth Night' and 'The Merry Wives of Windsor'. For five hundred years, the archipelago has cultivated grape vines that are unique, thanks to a rootstock that is ungrafted. Since the islands are relatively isolated, a ravenous aphid called phylloxera that destroyed most grapevines in Europe in the 19th Century, has never taken hold. Most European vines are now grown onto American rootstocks to provide immunity, whilst vines in the Canary Islands are from ungrafted rootstock, which makes all the difference to the flavour of the wine.

Nowadays, most of the islands' wine is drunk by its vast numbers of tourists, as well as the locals. However, some wine continues to be exported, particularly to the USA, where it is regarded very much as a wine for the connoisseur. Most of the islands' wine production comes from Lanzarote and Tenerife, but with an increasing output from the islands of Gran Canaria, La Gomera, El Hierro and La Palma. It is true that some of the islands are too hot and humid for the growing of grapes, but each of the islands have their own micro climates and individual typology that makes the growing of wine not only possible, but successful. Vineyards based within a lunar like terrain, such as on the island of Lanzarote, or small stone terraced vineyards at high altitudes, together with volcanic soil adds to the flavour of the islands' aromatic wines.

Not all attempts at producing wines have been successful. One enterprising vineyard, for instance, began to produce a sparkling wine in response to local demand. It was a banana-based wine, and a logical step since many bananas are grown on the islands. Sadly, this imaginative project came to an abrupt end, because many bottles started to explode as a result of on-going fermentation.

I visit each of the Canary Islands in turn each year and make a point of trying at least one of the local wines; I have yet to be disappointed. So, if on holiday in the Canary Islands, do add a little uniqueness to your holiday. Instead of ordering that usual bottle of

Rioja, do be a little more adventurous and try a bottle of wine produced in the Canary Islands; you won't regret it, but don't feel obliged to join in with the sex parties, unless you really want to!

Island Pride

Visitors to the Canary Island of Gran Canaria may be forgiven for thinking that it is a non-stop party island. The recent successful vote in Ireland for equal marriage, the Eurovision Song Contest and Maspalomas Pride have created an atmosphere of one long, heady party. The Canary Islands are blessed with one of the best climates in the world, which lends itself to an endless succession of parties and outdoor living. However, I can assure readers that we do get down to doing some work as well, but at our own pace.

Maspalomas Pride, which is often billed as 'the largest Pride event in Europe', once again drew thousands of gay, lesbian, bisexual, transsexual, and transgendered visitors to the island from all over Europe and further afield. There were also huge numbers of straight visitors too; many having visited in earlier years, and had such a good time that they come again each year to relive and share the experience.

Maspalomas Pride is a huge two-week party, with many spin off events, but above all it is a time to demonstrate equal rights, tolerance and equality, as well as a time to remember that respect and acceptance are not concepts yet shared across the world. The rainbow flag remains the centrepiece of the celebrations to remember those people across the world that still suffer from appalling discrimination and cruelty. Maspalomas Pride seeks to celebrate and give thanks for the freedoms enjoyed in Spain and the Canary Islands, as well as other countries that respect this equality. This event was one of the biggest Pride events ever seen on the island, with more than 80,000 visitors and residents lining the parade route.

Visitors often ask me why Gran Canaria, which is the third largest Canary Island by landmass, has become such a draw for gay and lesbian tourists. Gran Canaria has a well-deserved reputation for inclusivity and equality that has embraced gay and lesbian visitors for many years. People of all races, colour and religions live and work on the island and, in the main, happily coexist together. It is an island where the old adage 'live and let live' still strongly applies; as long as your activities don't hurt anyone else, then you are welcome. After visiting the island over many years, this was one of the main reasons that my partner and myself chose to move here; it was a decision that we have never regretted.

The Yumbo Centre, which is the main 'gay centre' and the centre for Pride is an uninspiring building, built 40 plus years ago as an arena. Over the years, it was slowly converted and now houses 40 plus gay bars, saunas, sex shops, drag shows, supermarkets, gadget shops, cafe bars and restaurants. To some, it looks like a badly worn multi-storey car park, which by day is a rather tacky commercial centre. However, by night, this uninspiring heap of concrete transforms itself into a throbbing and lively centre with something for everyone. From its early days, the Yumbo Centre became a beacon of hope for many gay men and women, and a place where they could relax and be themselves. It is a place where many relationships have begun, and ended, but above all it continues to be a place where gay men and women continue to feel safe, welcomed and valued.

So how did all this begin? I recall a conversation that I had with an elderly man, an ex-soldier, many years ago when I first visited the island. He told me that during the Spanish Civil War, the dictator, General Franco, would exile any soldier who was found to be gay to an island penal colony that was far away from the Spanish mainland; that island was Gran Canaria.

As the Pride procession and parties take place, my mind often goes back to this story and the fight for equality that has taken place over the centuries in Spain, as well as elsewhere in the world. The fight for equality and acceptance continue, but I am sure that those exiled Spanish soldiers would be very impressed with the part that this small island in the Atlantic has played in the fight for equality and justice for all.

A Bit of a Do

Have you noticed how many British youngsters, as well as the 'not so young', like to spend a few days soaked in a muddy field listening to their favourite bands nowadays? It is a pastime that has never really appealed to me since I am not that fond of tents, muddy fields, or having my eardrums shattered. However, I do understand something of the magical atmosphere that draws crowds to such well-established events as Glastonbury and many others that pop up throughout the year in the UK. I guess it is one of those things that you are supposed to do and say you enjoy, although at the time you really wish you had access to a hot bath and decent meal.

Of course, the Spanish have been enjoying festivals and fiestas for years, and can celebrate with a vengeance. Frankly, you name it and there is a patron saint, a fiesta or an event that you can use as an excuse to dress up, drink too much and generally have a good time whilst celebrating the wine harvest, the tomato crop or really anything that comes to mind.

One really good fun evening is the wine fiesta at Jumilla where one of the highlights over the weekend is the 'Gran Cabalgata del Vino' where hundreds of barrels of locally produced wine are poured over the participants. Basically, the tradition is that you turn up wearing white, and you end the evening looking something like a squashed tomato. Showers are kindly provided by the organisers. Mind you, although it is a wine festival, I am not sure that it shows the local brew in a particularly good light if it is only good enough to pour over the revellers. Just imagine doing that with a good Rioja!

Another bit of harmless fun is the 'Garachio Tyre Burning Fiesta', which comes courtesy of the Canary Island of Tenerife. Although it is a good headline grabbing title, it has more to do with dried corncobs soaked in petrol, balls of sackcloth, pineapples in wooden barrels, as well as burning tyres. This particular event re-enacts the fury of the Trevejo Volcano that destroyed the port of Garachio in 1706. Fireworks and glowing balls rolling down the slope help to recreate the effect of a volcanic eruption. Apparently, it is an amazing sight, but does very little to reduce levels of global CO_2 emissions.

Of course, among all the weird and loony events are those that glorify cruelty to the extreme, including bull running where terrified animals are let loose through some Spanish village streets with 'brave young men' running in front them, displaying their 'bravery and prowess' to all those who are prepared to witness this appalling act of cruelty. Some would say, fortunately, nine human participants have been gored to death so far this year, and I certainly find it hard to find sympathy for any of them.

On a lighter note, one of my favourites is the White Party that is popular at the beginning of Lent, and particularly on the Island of La Palma, although it has now sneaked into the party agenda for a number of other towns too. At this party, you turn up in white clothes, and unlike the Wine Festival, go home looking even whiter! You just have prepared to be doused in white powder, be it flour or talcum, to have a really good time.

Buzzing Around

The Canary Islander

"Love Me, Love My Thorax"

It is always good to hear of new visitors enjoying our wonderful island. However, I guess it is even better to learn about a resident that has been lurking on the island for thousands of years; not the same one, of course, but a family member.

No, I am not talking about some ancient drag queen, who is suddenly discovered in an embalmed condition in the cellar of a long forgotten show-bar in Playa del Ingles, but a new species of beetle. Love them or hate them, beetles (not drag queens) are all part of the Canary Islands' package of experiences, alongside cockroaches, millipedes and spiders. This new species of beetle is called Oromia thoracica, not the catchiest name I grant you, but the people who study such things can be a tad boring when it comes to catchy sounding names. It is a blind weevil that lives beneath the depths of the Agaete Valley, to the north-west of Gran Canaria. This area has some of the oldest soil on the island, somewhere between 5 and 23 million years old, but it is hard to be accurate about such matters, which can be irritating for those who like detail.

This new beetle, now commonly known as Thor, popped into the radar in the subsoil in this fertile valley about six years ago. Traps were duly laid, but Thor and his kind are canny creatures that deceived the investigators until recently when five of them fell into a trap following a heavy night out on the town. When they awoke two days later, it was too late, because the scientists had discovered them and, sadly, they were popped into a collecting jar.

Now this is the part where it all gets a little personal. What Thor lacks in size, since he is not a big boy at less that five millimetres long, he gains in his extremities that are longer and flatter than his cousins. This is actually a very useful attribute, because it means that Thor and his family can adapt more easily to life in their underground environment and narrow cracks, where headspace is at a bit of a premium. Thor and his family are blind, but are all dressed in rather natty reddish-brown jackets, which is typical of subsoil insects.

The clever thing about Thor is his thorax, which extends over his head as a sort of heart shaped shield, perfect for the more romantically inclined mate, which makes him unique from other species, but his opening line of "Love me, love my thorax", can be a little daunting to a potential mate. When it comes to fine dining, forget it, because Thor indulges in the rotting roots of bushes prevalent in the Agaete Valley, which makes him cheap, if not boring, to feed. Still, if you are looking for a cheap night out...

Apparently, the underground world of Gran Canaria is still a bit of a mystery, but there are many more surprises in store, to which I am sure many of our visitors will testify. However, I am referring to biodiversity, since the island is considered to be a real hotspot for future discoveries. I am told that a new species is discovered on the island every six days or so, which is an amazing statistic. Meanwhile, I wish Thor and his family well, but he should warn the rest of his species to keep away from the traps that lie in wait in the Agaete Valley.

Robins and Canaries

I am sure that I heard and saw a robin today. It is not a sight that I have seen since living in the UK, but I could not mistake its cheery voice and bright red breast. I watched this cheerful visitor for a few seconds as it sat on a tree watching me put rubbish into the bin before it flew off. It was a welcome sight and brought back many happy memories. This brief incident set me thinking about another bird, which I am often asked about, and that is the canary.

I am often asked why canaries are not seen flying wild in the Canary Islands. After all, surely the Canary Islands are the home of this popular (usually yellow) chirpy little bird with the wonderful voice? Thankfully, keeping one as a pet indoors is not as popular in the UK as it once was, but they are still very popular pets in many Spanish homes. Indeed, many visitors assume that our group of islands close to the coast of Africa are named after the canary bird, when it is really the other way around.

I hate to shatter too many illusions, but this beautiful little bird has very little to do with the Canary Islands. However, you may see a solitary canary, stuffed into a cheap cage that is far too small for it, baking alive on the balcony of one of the many apartments on the island. Those bought as a King's Day gift for granny, will usually be long dead by Easter, but never mind, in this consumer based, recession hit society, where animal welfare is a very low priority, a replacement can always be bought for granny next year...

The Canary Islands are derived from the Latin name, Canariae Insulae, which means the Island of Dogs. Canis in Latin means dogs, and it is thought that when one of the islands, Gran Canaria, was rediscovered by Roman sailors, it was inhabited by a species of very large wild dogs. Another theory is that the large dogs were actually monk seals, a species that is no longer present in the Canary Islands. To add to the confusion about the name and the accuracy of the 'dog story', historical accounts show that when the Spanish conquered the islands, there was no sign of the large dogs, yet the term 'Islas Canarias' was a name to remain until the present time. Interestingly too, this name was originally only given to the island of Gran Canaria; it was not a collective name for the group of seven inhabited islands as it is today.

Another theory is that the original inhabitants of the islands, the Guanches, worshipped dogs, which they regarded as holy animals. Some theories speculate upon the possible connection between the worship of these large dogs by the Guanches and the Egyptian cult of the dog headed god, Anubis. Indeed, the link with dogs, and not canaries, continues to be represented in the islands' coat of arms. Another, less romantic story, maintains that the name of the islands refers to the plant, Canaria, found in the Canary Islands, which was used to purge the bowels of dogs.

Visitors and bird watchers need not be disappointed, since there are references to around 420 species of birds to be found in the Canary Islands, of which eight species are globally threatened, and yes, there is a European Robin, and a Rufous-tailed Scrub Robin, to be found on the checklist of birds in the Canary

Islands, albeit with labels of 'rare/accidental', so maybe it was not the influence of festive cheer after all. In my case, the visitor was a European Robin, and I felt very fortunate to witness such a sight, and on Christmas Day too.

The canary bird is therefore named after the islands and not the other way around as many think. Sadly, visitors will not see bright yellow canaries flying around the islands, or maybe if they do, they will have been one of the fortunate ones to escape from their tiny prisons on the hot balconies. It always makes me wonder why they bother to sing at all.

Barbecue or What?

It is often said that we go around with our eyes closed, and it seems that I am no exception. It is also certainly true that it sometimes takes showing visitors around the area where we live before we truly appreciate and understand what we have close by.

Walking our dog, Bella, recently with a good friend who was visiting the island led us to an area where we have walked many times by the sea before. In the distance was what I always thought to be a barbecue area, mainly because of the barbecue shaped concrete object in the distance, complete with chimney, that I have seen so many times before in official picnic and barbecue areas in Spain. Sadly, I had never bothered to investigate further.

It was only when our friend commented that what I had previously thought was a barbecue is, in fact, a 'Trig Point'. I was vaguely aware of these objects, correctly named as triangulation points in the UK, but was not aware of seeing one in the Canary Islands, and I certainly did not expect to find one so close to home. In the UK, these trig points are concrete pillars used by the Ordnance Survey to discover the exact shape of the country. They are usually to be found at high levels of ground to allow for a direct line of sight from one trig point to the next. The top of the pillar is designed to allow for a theodolite (a kind of protractor built into a telescope) to be sited so that an accurate angle may be measured – a process called 'triangulation'.

The Ordnance Survey maps that are still lovingly used in the UK today were the result of a project that began in 1935, to accurately map out the shape of the country. The series of coordinates displayed is known as the 'National Grid'. The process appears to have been one of dedication and immense skill, since they claim an accuracy of just 3mm across the entire length of the country. Aerial photography, digital mapping and GPS measurements have largely superseded this process and, sadly, some of these trig points are disappearing or have fallen into disrepair.

The UK was not the only country to use this system of mapping, and many examples can be found in countries across the world. In Spain, there are over 11,000 triangulation stations erected by the Instituto Geografico Nacional (http://www.ign.es). These are usually made up of a cylinder, some 120 cm high and 30 cm diameter on a concrete base. The trig point close to our home in Gran Canaria is of similar design, and was erected in July 1991. Whilst it could do with a bit of a makeover, it is reassuring to know that it is part of a nationwide network and that our islands were not forgotten.

I will now be much more alert to find other trig points on Gran Canaria, as well as the other islands that we visit. The history and use of triangulation points is an interesting subject and I was delighted to discover that it was not just another barbecue.

The Disgruntled Expat

I had dinner with George again last week. As regular readers will probably remember, George is an elderly friend of ours, whom we have known for many years. I sometimes wonder why I bother with George, since he spends most of his time complaining. George will complain about anything, including 'the natives', as he calls them, the Spanish language, food, health service and the weather. I often wonder why George did not pack up and head back to his home town of Preston in the UK many years ago, such is his distain for all things 'foreign'. George is a 'professional complainer'; however, when I am in the mood, I do find him amusing and it always provides a healthy balance to my own rather more optimistic view of expat life.

George grunted as he sat down in his least disliked restaurant, as I made my first mistake of asking him how he was. We then spent a good fifteen minutes discussing his various ailments, his feet, his heart, his doctor, the hospital and the ambulance service before, thankfully, our starters arrived.

For a few minutes, George was silent as he began to tackle his prawn cocktail. He seemed to be enjoying it, although I could be wrong. Suddenly, he put down his fork, glared at me accusingly and asked, "What have you done to the weather?" I was a little taken aback, since weather control is not one of my jobs. "Well, I guess, it has been a little cooler than usual," I replied.

This was the response that George wanted and he began to recount news items and weather statistics, which claimed that it has been the coolest in the Canary Islands for at least 30 years. He hadn't come to the islands for this sort of treatment and he was actually thinking of returning to Preston.

"I'm going home," George announced in a deliberate voice. "I've had enough of all this nonsense. I can't stand the cold weather and the health service is going down the pan here. Do you know that I had to wait for two days to get an appointment to see the doctor? I could have died waiting all that time." I didn't like to tell him that some friends who had recently visited told us that they had to wait two weeks before they could see their doctor in the UK.

George was actually considering returning to his home town at the tender age of 80 plus. Since George has been threatening this in all the years that I have known him; it seemed highly unlikely. I said nothing, since I have risen to this bait many times before and have learned my lesson.

George did have a point. It has certainly has been a little cooler in the Canary Islands than normal this year, and the coolest January since 2006. Don't get me wrong, we have had some lovely warm, sunny days as well, with temperatures in the high teens and even low twenties, but it is certainly cooler than normal. Of course, expats and particularly those from the UK, continue to enjoy complaining about the weather, wherever they are. In fact, the cooler weather has provided endless entertainment and conversation for some, which I guess has been a blessing in many ways.

The main problem has been the wind, which I am told has been more than 35 per cent stronger than usual for this time of the year. The gusty wind has been cold, which has helped to bring down temperatures across all the islands.

Of course, the cooler weather is hardly noticed by our visitors from Scandinavia and Germany, who mostly spend their days in shorts and flimsy tops. Given that their countries are much colder, they do wonder what all the fuss is about. On a more positive note, our Canarian friends and neighbours tell us that they are enjoying the cooler weather, and wish that they could have more of it. You clearly cannot please everyone.

Returning to George, who had by now tackled most of his main course of roast beef and Yorkshire pudding, seemed disappointed at the long silence from me in response to his announcement.

"I'm going home. It's been a long time, but I've had enough," George repeated loudly, wiping horseradish sauce off his white beard.

"So when are you leaving, George? We really must meet up before you go. I'll help you to pack, if it will help."

"I'm not sure yet. I will probably wait until after my next hospital appointment, and I really would like to see a bit of Carnival. I'm also going on a day trip to one of the other islands, but I can't remember which one. I'll also need to find somewhere to live in Preston."

"Well, do your homework before you go, George." I added, seriously. "It's been a bit cold in Preston recently, so maybe you should wait until the better weather."

"Maybe you are right. I fancy a desert."

"Why not, George. Anyway, I hear that we are in for another lovely warm day tomorrow."

Strictly at the Bus Station

It was a very late night, or rather the early hours of the morning. It seemed that after a very good night with a leisurely dinner, a concert and a few drinks that we would have to wait a very long time for the next bus to our home in the south of the island. The bus station was deserted, our usual cafe bar closed many hours ago, the vending machine was out of order and what I really wanted was a long, cool drink of water. It was rare that we had experienced a time that was so quiet in Gran Canaria's impressive capital, Las Palmas, which as Spain's seventh largest city, we had always assumed was a city that never sleeps. This night was the exception.

We sat in the deserted bus station. Stretched out on one of the benches in the far corner was the shape of a body huddled beneath an old and dirty blanket; no doubt one of the many homeless people in the city who had decided to make the bus station a place of refuge until morning. It was going to be a long night.

As my ears adjusted to the near silence, I could hear the faint sound of lively music coming from the far end of the bus station. Maybe it was music playing from one of the many apartments in the area. I decided to investigate further, in the hope that I might find an all night cafe bar. As I walked towards the far end of the bus station, the music became louder and louder, and I could see that the lights were on. Yes, it was a bar, and the good news was that it was still open. I could get a bottle of water, and maybe a coffee.

Peering through the haze of smoke inside the bar, I could see many people laughing, talking and dancing. As my eyes adjusted to the light and dense smoke, I could see that many people were dancing in the centre of the room in what served to be a makeshift dance floor. Small tables and stools around the edge were filled with middle aged and elderly men and women chatting to each other. It was as if I had suddenly stepped back in time. I could see men, as well as women, smoking cigars as well as cigarettes. Since the law banning smoking in bars came into force, this was a sight that I had not seen for some time, although I am well aware that small bars, and particularly those open late at night still flout the law, when the owners perceive that they can get away with it.

It was traditional music and dancing, together with strumming guitars, and stomping feet that captivated my attention. It was a little like experiencing a small bar in Havana during one of those films set in Cuba in the 50s and 60s, yet with more than a hint of TV's 'Strictly Come Dancing'. However, this time there were no glitter balls, sequins, flowing flamenco dresses, or talkative judges holding scorecards, but an earthy combination of cigar smoke and sweat. Although trainers and jeans were mostly the order of the day, several woman and men wore sturdy shoes with impressive heels that gave the impressive click that their dance steps demanded.

Although I am not a dance expert, thanks to 'Strictly Come Dancing' I could recognise Flamenco, the Paso Doble and Bolero. There were others that I did not recognise, including one where several couples joined hands and danced in a circle, which I was told by one couple was a traditional dance from Catalonia, the Sardana.

I watched the scene unfolding with an increasing degree of admiration for the older members of the group. Certainly, some looked quite infirm, with a few relying upon walking sticks. However, even they took part in the slower numbers, albeit unsteadily. In their minds, they had become young and healthy once again. What a tonic!

I felt a little like Doctor Who, slipping through a vortex in time to discover something new and exciting that appears only now and again, or maybe I am thinking of Brigadoon? I glanced at my watch; it was time to catch the next bus home. I would love to have stayed longer to witness even more 'Strictly at the Bus Station'.

Travelling Back in Time

Visitors often forget that there is much more to the island of Gran Canaria than sunshine and beautiful beaches. Brits, Germans and Scandinavians flock to the Canary Islands in search of the sunshine and warmth that they have been missing during the winter months in their home countries. Desperate to squeeze in as many sunshine hours that they can, many tourists shy away from looking at the islands' ancient past, visiting traditional Canarian villages, exploring the mountain areas and learning more about the islands' ancient past. The same too can be said of many of us who live on the islands. It is often only when visitors arrive that we are reminded that our islands contain many treasures to explore, and forces us away from our daily routines.

One such island treasure is the Painted Cave of Galdar (La Cueva Pintada de Galdar), which can be found to the North of Gran Canaria. Galdar was the centre of the rulers of the Guanches, the original inhabitants of Gran Canaria, before the Spanish conquest of the island. In a small cave in the town, the Guanches painted intricate geometric paintings that depicted much of the routine and rituals of their daily lives. In island aboriginal culture, painting the walls of caves was common practice and this is one of the best-preserved examples of rock art that can be seen anywhere. Following the Spanish conquest in 1478, the Spanish invaders built a new city and the original Guanche settlement disappeared and the painted cave was lost.

In 1873, a local man clambered through a narrow gap

in the rocks and discovered the cave and the paintings. Word quickly got around and soon many people were visiting the cave where mummified bodies, Guanche pottery and tools were also found. The cave was finally opened to the public about one hundred years later, but this led to an increase in sunlight and humidity, which caused the paintings to deteriorate. In 1982 the island government closed all public access to the caves until a way to preserve this valuable heritage could be found.

Many years later, the Cueva Pintada was once again opened to the public, together with a modern visitor centre that provides helpful background information about the life of the Guanches. Visitors are now able to explore this fascinating Canarian aboriginal village, which is an amazing testimony to an ancient and ancestral civilisation. The Guanches lived in cave houses, and used Stone Age tools to cut and shape the rooms from the soft volcanic rock. They built walls from basalt without the use of mortar, and carved beds and seats from the soft rock. This early human settlement has now been professionally excavated and the entire site is covered to protect the excavations, as well as controlling light and humidity that can cause so much damage.

You can visit the Cueva Pintada, which is recognised as one of the most important archaeological sites in the Canary Islands, and tours are given in several languages. So, if you plan to visit the island, and get tired of the sun and lazing by the pool, just head off to Galdar and invest in a trip through the past. You won't regret it.

Lavender Lemonade and Biscuits

One of our neighbours, Noelia, called to see us a few days ago, and I was a little taken aback when she pounced upon the lavender growing vigorously in our garden. Noelia excitedly pointed at the plants and told me that she had tried growing lavender on many occasions, but without success and couldn't understand why our plants were full of bloom and giving off a heady perfume, when after all, she only lived a few doors away. I am no gardening expert, so didn't really have a ready answer, but promised to try to grow some cuttings for her. It was a promise that I then immediately regretted, since I have never grown cuttings from lavender before.

Gardening and plants have always given me a lot of pleasure, and I have been working quite hard recently to improve our small garden. It has taken a few years to get around to developing it as I would like, mainly because I have been waiting to complete a long awaited extension, which would also mean digging up well established existing trees and shrubs, and a job that I have to admit to putting off. However, the main work has now been done and I can concentrate on developing a garden that is easy to maintain, but also to reflect my love of a few special plants to remind me of our home in the UK, as well as Canarian plants that I know will grow well in the hot, often arid conditions of the south of Gran Canaria where I live.

One of the plants that I knew would grow easily in the Canary Islands and Spain is lavender. From my experience in the UK, I knew that once it is established it is relatively trouble free, its heady scent wards of some of the nasty insects and it would flower with ease until it grew too 'woody' and would have to be dug up.

It was during my research into how to successfully grow cuttings for Noelia, that I discovered that lavender is part of the mint family, and is actually native to the Canary Islands, as well as the South of France, so I am surprised that I do not see more plants growing in gardens and on patios. Its beautiful purple blooms, silver foliage and heady perfume make it an ideal garden plant. Bees love it too, and although some regard it as a short-lived plant, I have had the same plants flowering freely for many years, albeit with the occasional dramatic prune when it starts to look too 'woody'.

I also grow lavender in pots on our patio, as well as planted in the garden, and began to wonder why our plants have been so successful, whereas Noelia's plants died. I suspect it is due to poor drainage, since these plants do best, and produce more scented oil, in dry soil. I use a simple watering system beneath the soil that operates for only two minutes, twice a day, and so the plants never have too much water, and both garden and pot plants are planted in gritty soil to provide good drainage.

Noelia also told me that one of the reasons why she wanted to grow lavender was to collect the flower sprigs and to dry them for use in her home. In addition, Noelia wanted to add lavender to freshly made lemonade to add flavour, as well as adding it to home made biscuits. I am not at all sure about this, because as much as I like the plant, and appreciate its perfume for warding of mosquitoes and other nasty insects, I don't think I would appreciate too much of the perfume indoors, nor am I too keen on Noelia's idea of drinking or eating the plant. If anyone does try this, do please let me know the outcome, but do only use lavender that has not been treated with garden chemicals.

The Robinson Crusoe Experience

Islands have always fascinated me, and I also love a good story, which is probably why one in particular sticks in my mind. That book is Daniel Defoe's Robinson Crusoe, which was first published in 1719. It is the story of a castaway who spends thirty years on a remote tropical island. It is hardly a carefree holiday for the poor man, since Crusoe has to contend with mutineers, captives and cannibals before he is finally rescued.

The exact location of Robinson's Crusoe's island has always been a bit of a mystery, with many saying that the story is based on an island off Chile, some refer to Fiji, whilst others believe that a tiny Canary Island was the setting. I have even read an account that claims it was based in Cornwall. Initially, readers thought that the book was an autobiography, but it was later discovered that the story was based on the life of Alexander Selkirk, a Scottish castaway, who lived for four years on the Pacific Island called 'Más a Tierra', which is now part of Chile. To add to the confusion, the country's tourism chiefs cleverly changed the name to Robinson Crusoe Island in 1966. No doubt Defoe intended the book to be just a good story and not an exact account of a real life incident, and so I guess the location is really one based within the reader's imagination.

Personally, I like to think it is the Island of La Graciosa, a small Canary island, just a short ferry ride off the coast of the island of Lanzarote. Most of the island's current visitors are those from neighbouring Canary Islands and Spanish holidaymakers. La

Graciosa, and 'Gracious' it certainly is, is a small, volcanic island, and one of the very few places where there are no tarmac roads, just white sandy tracks; to use the old cliché, it is just like stepping back in time. The island and nearby islets form part of the Chinijo Archipelago Marine Reserve, which is the largest marine reserve in Europe, as well as being an area of exceptional landscape value and beauty.

Motor vehicles are strictly prohibited on La Graciosa, other than a few special purpose vehicles. The island has a small community of around 700 people living there, supplemented by a steady stream of day-trippers. There are few shops, and even fewer restaurants. Indeed, in typical post World Financial Crash fashion, its only bank closed a few years ago. It is not an island to visit if your main interest is shopping and nightlife. However, if you like visiting beautiful deserted beaches, walking, cycling and admiring breath-taking views, this little treasure could be just the thing to help blow away the stress accumulated from the outside world.

I doubt that many will find their 'Man Friday' on the island, since the nightlife is pretty poor, and the cannibals left long ago. However, if you do visit one day, I am certain that it will be a visit to remember. Now, do please keep all this information quiet, because the island really is a well-kept secret, and we don't want too many to know about it, do we? Meanwhile, do dig out that old copy of Robinson Crusoe.

Beware of Visitors Wearing Black and Yellow Striped Shirts

One of my pet hates are people who announce loudly to anyone who will listen that they don't like hospitals or funerals. Come off it, who does? It is a pointless and unnecessary comment. After all, the only people who like hospitals and funerals are, I suspect, morticians and funeral directors in the case of funerals, and doctors and nurses in the case of hospitals. For the general population, most of us like to steer well clear of both of them, until our time comes, which it inevitably does. Meanwhile, most of us like to just get on with our lives as best we can.

I am similarly irritated by the comment that "I don't like wasps"; after all, is there anyone who genuinely likes wasps? I guess they are an acquired taste. However, I fully accept that many people have genuine phobias of various insects ranging from spiders, daddy long legs and cockroaches, as well as wasps. I also know from personal experience that wasps, for some people, can be very dangerous, since one of my parents' friends died of a wasp sting some years ago.

It was within this context that I tried to frame a friendly and informative reply to an email from a potential holidaymaker that I received last week, asking if there are any wasps in the Canary Islands. Frankly, I have never seen a wasp in Gran Canaria, although I have seen plenty of honey and other varieties of bees in our garden. It is also sometimes difficult to briefly distinguish between a wasp and a honeybee unless at very close range. I wondered why wasps are avoiding the Canary Islands, because I know that there are wasps in Morocco, which is not that far away, and the fruit cultivation on these islands would suggest that there must be the occasional wasp ready to chance his luck.

Questions to friends in Lanzarote and Fuerteventura brought similar responses about the absence of wasps on these islands. It was only after checking with a friend on the small island of La Gomera, that I was reminded of an incident a couple of years ago when a giant wasps' nest was discovered in San Sebastian de La Gomera. Police had to break into an empty house after receiving complaints from neighbours. There they found the mother of all wasps' nests that was 7 metres long. Migratory wasps from Africa occupied the nest, after all the islands are only 100 kilometres from Morocco by sea, and the native variety would not build a nest of such a large size. The nest almost filled the room and contained millions of wasps, which may well be a candidate for the Guinness Book of Records, as being the largest wasps' nest ever found.

Back to the email from the wasp-hating potential visitor. I suspect that the Canary Islands are as good as it gets for wasp-hating visitors. Maybe I can only answer that seeing or being attacked by wasps on the islands is extremely unlikely, but to avoid visiting derelict and empty buildings on La Gomera.

There's Nothing Grotty About Lanzarote!

It is strange how names, derogatory or otherwise, tend to stick in the mind for a long time. Many years ago, the only thing I knew about Lanzarote was the reference to 'Grotty Lanzarote' by a friend who at the time worked for a tour operator, but later found his niche in life as a fireman. Despite his lack of success as a tour operator, I was still intrigued to visit Lanzarote, and find out the truth for myself.

Since that time, I have visited the island many times and it has grown to become one of my favourite islands. Each of the Canary Islands is unique in their own spectacular and special way, but Lanzarote appeals particularly to my sense of order, with an environment that is appealing to the eye. I love the fact that there are no high rise buildings blotting its spectacular landscape, and its many quaint towns and villages that retain so much of their past, with neat, white painted buildings and clean litter-free pavements. Unlike many other towns and villages on these islands, those on Lanzarote appear to have been planned, and not thrown together and grown aimlessly into a 'topsy turvy' mass of all types of buildings and structures.

Much of the gratitude for the development and planning on the island has to be given to the island's son, César Manrique, a painter, sculptor and architect; a genius of a man whose life and work had such an overpowering influence on the island, which continues to the present time. His interventions to ensure that development fitted into a unique landscape continue to be a heritage that the island is rightly proud of. Visiting the island again recently, I found it hard to believe that César Manrique was killed in a car crash in 1992; such is his continued influence and presence upon present day Lanzarote.

Lanzarote is the most easterly of the Canary Islands, being only 100 kilometres from Africa and 1000 kilometres from Peninsular Spain. The island has a very distinctive character shaped by the natural forces of earth, wind and fire. As well as pure Saharan sand on its beautiful beaches, there are dramatic volcanic landscapes and gentle hills that can only be described as 'bumps'. The island is volcanic, with volcanoes that are still alive, but quaintly described as "sleeping", with the last eruptions taking place in the 18th Century. However, there is still some volcanic activity, with hot points that can reach 100-120 ºC on the surface and 600ºC at only 13 metres from the surface, so be careful where you place your hands.

Somehow, Lanzarote has escaped over-development and a 'lager lout' culture that beset many such destinations. There is a sense of civilisation even in the small, elegantly developed, tourist areas. The streets show little sign of dog poo, litter or chewing gum that could so easily destroy its clean and tidy image. If you are looking for a party island, or one for a lively stag or hen 'do', or an all action holiday for the kids, forget Lanzarote. However, if you are looking to refresh the soul and enjoy a quiet, relaxing time on an island that knows how to welcome visitors, I suggest that you give this beautiful island a try. Over the years I have come to realise that the description of "Grotty Lanzarote" could not be further from the truth.

How Not To Do It!

The Canary Islander

"We're all-inclusive" – Set yourself free!

The newly elected President of the Canary Islands produced a very good sound bite last week, no doubt knowing that it would go down exceedingly well with most businesses on the island that cater for tourists. Basically, he was saying that hotels that offer all-inclusive deals to their guests are doing a great disservice to the islands. It is one of those sound bites that nearly everyone on the island will have sympathy with, other than the internationally owned hotels and tour companies that sell such deals. It is something that most of us have been saying for years, since the popularity of 'all-inclusive' holidays took off.

Essentially, all-inclusive hotel deals do very little to help the local economy. It is true that some of the money paid to hotels finds its way into the pockets of hotel staff, and maybe some local produce. However, the profits are sucked overseas into the companies that own the large hotel chains and do very little to benefit the islands. This is cash that visitors are not spending in local restaurants and bars and, as such, many excellent venues are closing, or are in deep trouble.

From the alternative point of view, I can appreciate that the elderly, and families with children may appreciate the benefits of an all-inclusive deal. Elderly folk, in particular, may not want the bother, or have the energy to find a restaurant in the evening and we all know how quickly kids can run up the bill with ice creams, colas etc. In the 'Benidorm style' world, the 'all-inclusive' wrist tag means that there are no concerns about unexpected expensive, large restaurant and bar bills; everything is paid for before departure, and visitors can, in theory, arrive without a euro in their pocket for the duration of their holiday.

Many of our friends who stay in hotels on the island do so on a half board or bed and breakfast basis, leaving them free to explore local restaurants in the evening. This offers a choice of local cuisine, variety and an experience that many will see as the point of going on an overseas holiday. Other friends who book an 'all-inclusive break' are usually restricted to the time that they can eat, and avoid eating out elsewhere in the evening simply because they have already paid for it. They also claim "We cannot eat lunch, because we will be eating a big meal this evening, which we have already paid for". These restrictions tend to take the sparkle and variety out of a holiday, and reduce the flexibility that a holiday should provide. Simply because it is 'free' and we can eat and drink as much as we like may not be the best way to enjoy the holiday experience. In their defence, some will say that by eating in their hotel they can be assured of the same quality throughout the holiday. Maybe, but isn't exploring, making decisions, trying out new things and enjoying different surroundings all part of the holiday experience? Does collecting almost the same meal from the all-inclusive buffet each evening and returning to table 63 offer the same experience?

Despite the disadvantages of going all-inclusive, many local restaurants and bars have their issues too. Irregular pricing, unduly variable food quality and service are all issues that require continual monitoring and correction. We noticed this on our own recent holiday, which was bed and breakfast only; we found great difficulty finding a restaurant that would cater for a specific diet, in our case vegetarian. Despite a good number of restaurants, most were closed on Mondays, either because it was their day off, or closed for a week or two for seasonal holidays. Maybe a little local coordination would have tempted visitors to stay in the town to eat. As a result, we had little alternative but to eat in the hotel on two evenings, since the only option was a long taxi journey to another town to find a restaurant that was open.

Despite the President's words, it is not a black and white issue. Visitors have the right to spend their hard earned cash as they wish. Local restaurants and bars should play their part, cut out complacency and make every effort to make visitors want to eat in their premises. The successful ones will succeed, and the half-hearted ones will fail. As for holidaymakers, please give local bars and restaurants a chance. Liberate yourself, be brave and throw away that plastic 'all inclusive' wristband for a few days. As far as the Canary Islands are concerned, I doubt you will regret it.

What an Inconvenience!

Witnessing a group of scantily-clad angels with wilting wings relieving themselves against a tree in Las Palmas during Carnival, brought home to me that the city has nowhere near enough public toilets. In fact, I would be hard pressed to name one, other than in the bus station and museum. When I say angels, I should point out that it was not the heavenly host who had lost total control of their bladders, but a group of revellers dressed as angels. I suspect that the problem was that it was 3.00am, and they were full of the local brew, which was being freely distributed during the Parade.

Now, I realise that this is not the nicest subject to be taking about, but the fact is that, unlike Paris, Spain has very few public toilets. Indeed, a recent news item made the point that in Madrid, which has over three million residents and over 10 million annual visitors, there are only 25 public toilets (that is, if they are working), leaving many desperate to relieve themselves elsewhere. The few public toilets that are available are often either not working or closed from 9.00pm, which is not a great deal of help, since that is time when most people are just thinking about going out for the evening.

Of course, the idea is that the public should use facilities provided in bars and restaurants, which is fine if you stop and stay for yet another drink. Sadly, too many visits to bars for a drink and a pee mean the inevitable repeats itself before too long. Some cafe bars refuse entry to those only wanting to make use of their facilities, which leaves many - usually men -

relieving themselves against any available tree, wall and street light. Sadly, strolling around Madrid and other cities late in the evening can be an unsettling experience, with an overpowering stench of urine on many street corners.

Sometimes, of course, it is simply bad manners, because the offender cannot be bothered to find an alternative place to go to the toilet. Urinating in public is an offence in Spain, which can lead to a hefty fine. However, the police rarely impose this sanction. Incidentally, this law also covers spitting in public, which is good to know.

There we have it, if you are caught short in Spain, just head to the nearest cafe bar and, hopefully, they will take pity upon you without you having to resort to buying another drink. If you do not want another drink or do not have the cash, head to the local bus station, public library or museum, if it is open. You may even be fortunate enough to find one of those 'coin in the slot' loos, which are rare, but can be an interesting and challenging experience. However, do please read the instructions carefully first, which are available in a variety of languages. Alternatively, you could become a bus driver, which would entitle you to free use of the limited public facilities in Madrid. However, if you have a weak bladder, do avoid becoming a taxi driver, since there are no facilities provided and it can be a very long day.

Boozing Whilst Cruising

Judging from some of the expat correspondence that I have read recently, many of the more sober Brits are not too impressed to discover that many of their countrymen are so badly behaved in Spain that British policemen were sent over this season to several resorts to assist the Spanish police. Hailed as a "success" in Mallorca and Ibiza, Benidorm now wants to get in on the act and have British bobbies on the beat there too.

It seems that we are now entering a new phase in international relations since we cannot trust Brits to behave well abroad. British officers will now be sent to traditional party hotspots that are popular with young Brits. Apparently, "Seeing a British bobby patrolling the streets or on the beach helps tourists to feel at home," according to a Valencian regional spokesperson. That may be true, but how many Brits see a bobby patrolling the streets anywhere in the UK nowadays? It's years since this particular species were last seen patrolling the streets; after all, the weather is just too appalling to go outside. Maybe a holiday to a popular Spanish resort just to see a British bobby in action will become the latest tourist attraction?

Do British tourists really need to "feel at home" when on holiday? Surely, the point of going to another country for a holiday is to get away from home? Surely, British tourists are going to try real Spanish food, sample the superb wines, enjoy delicious tapas, traditional music and dancing? Sadly not, since although the TV comedy 'Benidorm' is meant to be a parody of Brits abroad, it is so funny, because it is actually true. The last thing a Brit on holiday in Benidorm, Mallorca or Ibiza wants is to be in a foreign country. Paella? You must be joking; its fish and chips that will really do the trick. A nice Spanish Rioja? Forget it; just hand over a pint of the local (preferably dirt cheap) brew. Tapas? Well, that's not proper food, is it? As for traditional music and dancing, no way! Lets just get bladdered and head off to the local disco pub.

Sadly, British police abroad will have no powers to arrest, but will serve "to remind British tourists the importance of observing local laws and customs," according to the rather pompous declaration from the British Embassy. Possibly this explains why two of the British officers sent under the trial scheme this summer were widely criticised in social media for observing local customs a little too much. Swimming with the tourists, taking selfies with holidaymakers, and with one officer reportedly participating in a boozy night out was maybe not the right way to start a new assignment as an ambassador and good example to fellow Brits.

One interesting aspect of the Benidorm scheme will be a system of exchange with officers from Spain's National Police going to areas of Britain where there are more Spanish nationals. What an excellent idea, which should mean one or two policemen on the beat. I have every respect for Spain's National Police, who are mostly very professional and well trained, but they are not to be argued with. It will be most interesting to see how they deal with offenders in the more notorious parts of Britain.

Meanwhile, readers will be pleased to hear that the latest crime wave to hit the streets of Benidorm, that of illegally riding mobility scooters, is going to be tackled more seriously in future. After all, being run down by a perfectly healthy, but inebriated teenager riding a mobility scooter may not the best way to start a holiday in the sun. In true 'Benidorm Madge' fashion, 'boozing whilst cruising' on such a vehicle will be frowned upon and 'booze filled' races will be crossing the line. In seems that the town has more than its fair share of disabled Brits visiting with over 500 mobility scooters on the resort's streets every day. These 'booze bikes' will now be banned for people under the age of 55 with no physical disability, with fines of 36 to 65 euros for those who ignore the ban. Madge certainly has a lot to answer for.

The End of the World?

As I write this, I can hear violent rumbles of thunder and see flashes of lightning outside on a wet and humid day, which is unusual for the Canary Islands in September. Quite a few soothsayers, mystics, religious fanatics and the like have been warning that the World will end in September, so maybe this is a sign of things to come. This is quite good to know since I am planning to delay repaying my hefty credit card holiday bill until after 1 October, just in case. Mind you, the religious cult leaders may well be right since we are already seeing signs of a total collapse of the civilised world as we know it.

Firstly, Jeremy Corbyn has just been elected as leader of the British Labour Party. Shock horror, democracy really isn't supposed to work in this way; after all, we really cannot allow ordinary people to ditch the 'austerity' word and choose a different path can we? Secondly, Jeremy forgot to sing 'God Save the Queen', since he was standing in respectful silence at a Battle of Britain remembrance service, remembering the fallen, and completely forgot to enter into the expected 'lustful singing' of the words of this inane song. If the truth be told, the Queen is probably really fed up with this mournful dirge and would prefer a rendering of something far jollier; I already have a number of suggestions. Then we have the audacity of this new Leader of the Opposition not being at all happy about kneeling before the Queen in order to take up his newly elevated position as a Privy Councillor. In the old days this serious affront to the monarch would certainly end up with a visit to the Tower for a spot of beheading; in these more enlightened times, maybe the Queen will agree to a simple handshake or a friendly kiss instead? It is already clear that important issues such as these completely overshadow the refugee crisis, food poverty, potential environmental catastrophe and several wars; the seriousness of which could well lead to the end of the World, and so we had better be prepared.

Over in Spain, we are having a few problems of our own. Can you believe that a Spanish reporter actually had the cheek to address King Felipe VI of Spain with the informal "tu" (meaning "you") instead of using the more formal language of respect, such as "usted". Now this really has upset the good people of Spain, because the TV reporter appeared to be just a little "too chummy" with his royal highness who, by all accounts is a very warm and friendly person, and someone that many would quite like to have a coffee with.

It was a serious interview in which the reporter asked the King about the Euro Basketball game last week, and how he had made time to cheer the basketball players in his busy schedule. The King didn't seem particularly worried about the informality of the question, and answered the interviewer's questions with a smile. Sadly, many Spanish people have not been so forgiving and the social networks were awash with remarks about the "lack of respect" shown by failing to use the formal tense of the language in such conversations. However, someone else kindly pointed out that the last journalist to call the King "tu" ended up marrying him. He was, of course, referring to

Queen Letizia, who was herself a journalist before she married King Felipe.

So to Jeremy Corbyn, and others in positions of authority, I would say that it is what is in your heart and mind that matters most, and that being a leader is not just about the procedures, pretences, formalities and traditions of the job, although I know that many will disagree. As for the end of the World, if my article does not appear next week you will know what has happened, but at least I will not have paid my credit card bill!

Printed in Great Britain
by Amazon.co.uk, Ltd.,
Marston Gate.